The Way We Work

The Way We Work

An Encyclopedia of Business Culture

Volume 2
M–Z

Edited by Regina Fazio Maruca

GREENWOOD PRESS
Westport, Connecticut • London

Library of Congress Cataloging-in-Publication Data

The way we work : an encyclopedia of business culture / edited by Regina Fazio Maruca.
   p. cm.
   Includes bibliographical references and index.
   ISBN-13: 978-0-313-33886-1 ((set) : alk. paper)
   ISBN-13: 978-0-313-33887-8 ((vol. 1) : alk. paper)
   ISBN-13: 978-0-313-33888-5 ((vol. 2) : alk. paper)
 1. Corporate culture—United States.   2. Work environment—United States.
I. Maruca, Regina Fazio.
HD58.7.W3328   2008
658—dc22   2007040510

British Library Cataloguing in Publication Data is available.

Library of Congress Catalog Card Number: 2007040510
ISBN: 978-0-313-33886-1 (set)
        978-0-313-33887-8 (vol. 1)
        978-0-313-33888-5 (vol. 2)

First published in 2008

Greenwood Press, 88 Post Road West, Westport, CT 06881
An imprint of Greenwood Publishing Group, Inc.
www.greenwood.com

Printed in the United States of America

The paper used in this book complies with the
Permanent Paper Standard issued by the National
Information Standards Organization (Z39.48–1984).

10 9 8 7 6 5 4 3 2 1

Contents

Alphabetical List of Entries

Entries by Subject

Preface

"Business Culture" isn't tangible. You can shape it; you can talk about its characteristics; you can describe how people who work in a certain office behave as a result of it; but business culture isn't something that can be physically grasped.

Accordingly, business culture is one of those "soft" yet incredibly powerful elements of business as a whole. The importance of business culture can perhaps be seen in the way it affects the individuals operating in that culture. A strong and positive business culture can foster growth in an organization and bring out the best in people. A weak culture, or a culture of intimidation, can cause initially productive employees to become disgruntled and unhappy to the point where they leave—it can also keep those who remain from forming the kinds of teams that win in the marketplace.

Culture can be the difference between a company where employees spend time together after work, and one where they all go their separate ways at 5 P.M. It can be the difference between a company where employees spend a great deal of time meeting secretively behind closed doors, and a company where they engage freely in a relatively tension-free atmosphere. Culture can be the difference between a company where employees compete against one another, and a company where employees share information and stand united, focused on external competition and on the customer rather than internal issues.

Importantly, culture can change on a dime. The culture of work is dynamic. A new chief executive officer (CEO) can change a company's culture pretty quickly. Similarly, a new manager can infuse a department with a particular culture. Employees at all levels shape the culture of their companies constantly by how they act, what they say to one another, and how they represent the company to customers.

When you step back and consider business culture as it applies to *all* companies—even if you set the boundaries loosely as "companies based in the United States" and then limit the scope to "office" work—you see that culture still evolves and changes, morphs and flows quickly at the big-picture level.

Knowing this, our goal in compiling *The Way We Work* was to offer our readers as many trends, definitions, and facts as possible within the covers of these two volumes in order to capture a colorful and varied freeze-frame look at office culture in the United States in the early years of the twenty-first century. It is our hope that the contents will resonate with the people who are hard at work in offices as of this writing, and help them better understand the forces and factors that influence their organizations. The set also offers a wealth of information that can serve as a useful resource and starting point for high school and college students who are entering the workforce and seek some guidance on what office work is like, and how it is evolving.

What You Will Find

Over 100 entries, ranging from American Association of Retired Persons (AARP) to white collar workers, and covering topics such as diversity, learning organizations, mission statements, the glass ceiling, generation X (Y, Z, etc.), and the war for talent, are included in this encyclopedia. The topics and terms have been selected because each of them, in some way, shapes the big picture of business culture as we know it.

It must be noted that one person's opinion of the kinds of things that shape business culture will naturally differ from someone else's. And opinions continue to change over time. In part, this transient nature of individual and general opinion is why a team of people including academic researchers, journalists, corporate coaches, and executives and employees from a wide range of companies came together to compile this book. In deciding what to include—and what not to include—the team engaged in often-vigorous debate over whether a certain term, or fact, or trend was really a "culture-shaper" and so belonged in these pages. The items selected for inclusion needed to have significant influence on business culture; they also had to have enduring impact. If you don't expect to see something, and it's included, that is because the team determined that the term or topic was in some way a significant influence on business culture. If you do expect to see something, and it's *not* here, that is most likely because some other term or topic beat it out in the final analysis. As a result, many formal and informal networks, associations, and the like are not called out in the A–Z listings; where possible, these have been included as reference sources.

In addition to the A–Z entries, you'll also find a set of short features titled "Why I Do This." These are personal narratives that tap into the motivations, pros, and cons of a host of individuals' career choices and in doing so move beyond office culture to include other kinds of work that enable and assist office culture. If you think you want to be a Web-marketing expert, there is a "Why I Do This" that offers a glimpse into what day-to-day life in this job is like. Are you more interested in working as a dental office manager? What about a career as a finance executive? Librarian? Or maybe a limo driver, enabling a host of executives, consultants, and the like to work in multiple locations with relative ease? Driving limos is not only about sitting in traffic; this job offers surprising upsides.

The "Why I Do This" essays do not represent every job available; what they offer, however, is an insider's perspective of the world of office work and its supporting services from a diverse group of people located across the United States. An outsider's view of what work in a given office is like can be vastly misleading; hearing directly from the employees is often an eye-opener.

The encyclopedia also contains several feature articles that speak to particular aspects of the culture of work. Some of these—including Rob Galford's essay on *Leadership Mindsets,* and Constantine von Hoffman's interview on *Blogs and Work*—were written for these volumes. Others, such as the articles reprinted from Knowledge@Wharton, an online resource offering business insights, analysis,and information from a variety of sources, have been included here because they offer particular insights into other cultural elements of office life, and because they bring dedicated research to bear on these issues.

The encyclopedia contains one key book chapter, reprinted from *Aligning the Stars* by Thomas Tierney and Jay Lorsch, and appearing here as an appendix. This piece provides an in-depth look at what culture means inside professional service firms. And a series of short pieces, appearing under the heading Signs of Changing Culture, reflect behaviors, happenings, trends, and other influences of culture as reported in major newspapers and magazines during the period when these volumes were being researched.

Finally, the bibliography represents a host of resources available for those who want to extend their research on business culture, or plumb the depths of one or another topic in particular.

Themes

Interestingly—though perhaps not surprisingly—across all of the elements in this work, several common themes emerge. Among them:

- An awareness of the social and environmental issues facing the world—poverty, inequality and global warming among them—and an increasing resolve to contribute to solutions.
- A continuing struggle over where the lines are and should be drawn with regard to the work/life balance. Can anyone who works in an office really "unplug" anymore? Should they?
- An awareness of the phenomenon of the "rise of the customer," or the increasing influence that consumers have on what companies make and market, and how responsive companies must be to consumers in order to succeed . . .
- A continuing and intensifying struggle to get the most out of human capital—people—in a competitive landscape where businesses increasingly compete in their ability to muster and channel talent.
- An ongoing effort to get Web-based business "right" including marketing, reach, and coordination with physical stores, so that companies don't compete against themselves in their online and physical worlds, and so that customers can expect to shop as easily whether they're on the computer or down town.

These themes and others are illuminated in related, cross-referenced entries in this work. They surface in the short, "Signs of Changing Culture" notes, and in the essays, interviews, and articles that flavor the encyclopedia throughout. They're also reflected in the "Why I Do This" narratives, to the extent that they have shaped people's expectations of the work they do, and the way in which they spend their days.

If You're Looking for a Job

One of the most interesting insights that surfaced during the process of putting together this encyclopedia is how different one job can be from another, even given the same necessary skills, and in many cases, the same job title. Culture is a prime differentiator. People with the "same" jobs at one company have profoundly different work experiences at another company, and sometimes, even when working for the same employer in different departments, or units, or functions.

This isn't really a surprising insight. But when you're faced with it, time and again, across the amount of information that gets considered for an encyclopedia, the range of different experiences, even given broad commonalities, is daunting.

The take-away from this insight is to search for the *culture* that fits an individual, not just one that works as a skills-match. There are any number of jobs out there that cause people to work in and around an office. But someone with financial skills can work for a zoo, or a bank, or a fire department, or an opera company, and have a profoundly different daily experience at work than their peers-in-skill work in other environments. Someone who works in human resources can be surrounded by lawyers, architects, consultants, cleaners, security guards, computer programmers, writers, designers, nurses, you name it. Again, while the job title may be the same, each alternative offers a different daily existence.

Extremes

While collecting and coordinating materials for this encyclopedia, we expected to find general themes. But many cultural "extremes" have also come to light. Job-seekers again take note. For example, consider the company whose top executive demands complete obedience from his employees—and also takes it upon himself to manage and support employees' personal lives, even offering marital and general life advice on a regular basis—the kind of company where employees call this senior leader in the middle of the night to discuss their personal lives. Or think about the insurance company that owns and stocks its own ponds, expects employees to spend time fishing, and allows them to keep what they catch. (This company also pays for a weight loss program; employees front some of the cost, but get their money back if they lose the weight they set out to lose. If not, the money goes to charity.)

These are merely samples of the individual cultures cultivated by certain companies. Scratch the surface of any company and you'll find unique cultural attributes. But scratch the surface of some, and you'll find "norms" that truly stand out.

Culture-Shaped Challenges

Our research also highlighted, time and again, the challenges and conflicts that make and break individuals, teams, and entire businesses, on any given workday. Battles rage over health care benefits, workplace standards, and equal employment opportunity. Tensions spiral out of control when directors and leadership teams clash over executive compensation, acquisitions, and divestitures. Bosses, peers, and direct reports face off over a market positions, pricing strategies, performance reviews, and the right way to make decisions. And all of these conflicts are framed and fueled by the culture at work in the organization at hand.

We hope that in these pages, you find resources that shed light on many different perspectives of "the way we work" and that the material herein informs your understanding of the forces shaping business culture, and opens new avenues of thought.

Wherever possible, we've included suggestions or links to additional information on any given topic for further research. We urge you to utilize these connections, and hope that you find them useful. Mostly, we hope you find what's in these pages interesting and provocative; we hope this encyclopedia encourages students and professionals alike to examine or re-examine their role or potential in the world of work as well as their contributions to business culture.

Acknowledgments

This work reflects the efforts of so many people—too many to name here. You know who you are. Your essays, your thoughts about business culture, your views about your own choice of jobs and careers, and your advice about sources and content are reflected on every page that follows. You have our profound and heartfelt gratitude.

We would like to recognize a few people explicitly, because of their unique and substantive contributions to this work:

Our thanks go to Nick Phillipson, who had the idea to do an encyclopedia of business culture designed primarily for students considering "office" work. His vision shaped the project from the early days; his thoughtful editing provided the guidelines for the encyclopedia's various elements.

Without Nick, the project would not have existed. Without Greenwood's Kristi Ward, it would not have been completed. Kristi stepped in at a crucial time to edit, to encourage, and literally to pull together and organize all of the many different editorial components that make up the whole. Her unflagging enthusiasm, her patience, and her expertise drove the project forward. She truly shouldered this encyclopedia and pushed it to completion.

Christine Marra's efforts were also utterly essential to the project's completion. Christine stepped in to edit the many alphabetical entries and other components of the encyclopedia. Her keen eye, efficient editing, and level-headed approach kept the project on track, and allowed us to picture what it would look like as a finished work, even when it was far from being finished.

Credit for the content in the A–Z entries goes largely to a team of skilled researchers, namely Marie M. Bell, Diane R. Walker, Catherine A. Cotins, and Rochelle Stewart. An encyclopedia requires researchers who are able to cast a wide net, assess a great deal of information, and select and present that which they believe really "captures" a definition succinctly and clearly. These folks were up to that task.

We would like to acknowledge, with deeply felt thanks, Sheryl Rowe's formidable editing and production skills, Bridget Austiguy-Preschel's production expertise, Megan Chalek's diligence and attention to detail, and the patience and skill of all of the other people who worked tirelessly behind the scenes at Greenwood to see this through.

Finally, our thanks as ever go to our families, for their patience, tolerance, encouragement and love.

Made in Japan

During the early part of the twentieth century the term "Made in Japan" or for that matter "Made in any other Asian country" was generally associated with cheap, unsophisticated products of inferior quality. At that time, consumers looking at a product label would see "Made in Japan" or China or India or some other country, and assume the product was poorly made. If their budget allowed for it, a consumer would almost certainly opt for an item of higher quality with the "Made in the USA" label. Following World War II, however, the stigma around "Made in Japan" began to evaporate with the rise of Japanese manufacturing expertise and by the 1970s a "Made in Japan" tag was associated with high quality, reliable products.

The transformation of Japan's manufacturing sector was the result of both circumstance and planning. During World War II, the Japanese economy was decimated and its manufacturing capacity almost literally flattened. Following the war, there was massive reinvestment in public and private infrastructure that created a "fresh start" for the business sector with new physical plants and the opportunity to institute new business practices. Additionally, the Japanese government created a group called MITI—the Ministry of International Trade and Industry. During the 1950s and 60s this group successfully focused on growth especially in the steel and shipbuilding industries.

The success in steel and shipbuilding was followed by subsequent wins in cars, electrical goods, precision products, and semi-conductors. Subsequent to the 1980s the Japanese economy experienced limited growth and the success of MITI as an agent of progress was questioned. For example, the *Wall Street Journal* noted (December 11, 1984), "A generation ago, Mr. Honda wanted to expand his motorcycle company by making cars . . . But they [MITI] wanted only two companies—Toyota and Nissan." Going against MITI policy, Honda went on to become not only a leading car maker but to create a path for other car manufacturers to follow.

Some of the world's most powerful consumer goods brand names today are Japanese, including Sony, Mitsubishi Electric, NEC, and Fujitsu. The success of the Japanese companies is often attributed to the product's customer driven design and reliability. In breaking into the U.S. markets, Japanese companies generally speaking, had limited access to service networks and therefore invested in product design, manufacturing processes, and management techniques that encouraged "built-in" reliability at reasonable prices. Goods that didn't break down as frequently required less service and therefore the Japanese companies did not need to build as extensive a service delivery network.

Increasingly there have been questions raised about what it means to be "Made in Japan." Like other manufacturers before them, Japanese firms have begun to manufacture their products outside of Japan. A Toyota vehicle purchased in the United States could probably have been assembled on a production line in the United States rather than actually made in Japan, though often the parts might have been made in Japan and the manufacturing techniques developed in Japan and then deployed at the local manufacturing site. The same can be said for an "American" car manufactured by Ford or GM where parts, design, and in some cases even assembly may have occurred outside U.S. borders.

Other nations, most notably Korea and other countries broadly described as the "Asian Tigers" have sought to replicate the Japanese success. In Korea, large family conglomerates called chaebols were useful "tools of government policy . . . providing lots of jobs and driving economic growth through exports" (*Economist*, April 22, 2006, page 63). Moreover, in doing so they became leaders in providing worldclass products to the world market; often in direct competition with Japanese firms. Leading the way are companies like Samsung in electronics and Hyundai-Kia in the automotive industry.

The most recent transformation has been "Made in China." Until relatively recently, like Japan before it, China's products had been viewed as price competitive at the expense of quality. That has changed within the decade. Unlike Japan that predominantly used capital investment to fuel its industrial rise, China, with its population of 1.3 billion—over four times that of the United States—has used labor as the driver of its economic engine. With labor costs about one-tenth that of an average U.S. worker, Chinese business has a competitive advantage, especially in labor intensive industries such as apparel and footwear. As the Communist government has loosened trade restrictions, China has benefited. As *Fortune* magazine noted (September 18, 2006), "In 2005, China exported $202 billion more to America than it imported, accounting for more than a quarter of the U.S. trade deficit."

An interesting consequence of China's industrial expansion has been its need for resources and its quest for them. The *Chicago Tribune* noted in December 2006:

> China had enough oil to sustain itself just fifteen years ago. Now it is one of the world's thirstiest oil addicts, importing 40 percent of what it needs. Only the United States consumes more. Each new factory churning out goods made in China and each new car on Chinese highways adds to a ravenous appetite for raw materials . . . satisfying that appetite has sent Chinese oil explorers around the world.

In addition to the competition for raw materials, the rise of Asian—and other regions—manufacturing has created a balance of payments deficit for the United States as Americans have purchased more imported products than it has exported to those countries. Several politicians and economists have expressed special concern about the increased negative balance of trade with China. Others, however, have noted that the U.S. consumers may have benefited as manufacturing has shifted to less expensive China from more expensive Asian locations. For example, the *New York Times* noted (September 7, 2006), "China may be good for our trade balance. American consumers seem determined to spend money, and Chinese businessmen have made the bill cheaper." In 1985, China, Japan, Hong Kong, Taiwan, and South Korea accounted for 52.3 percent of America's trade deficit. By 2005, this percentage had fallen to 40.9 percent, in part because of cost savings from buying Chinese.

See also: Just-in-Time

Further Reading

"Asia will Lose as 'Made in China' Goes Local," by Andy Mukherjee, Bloomberg .com, September 18, 2007. (www.bloomberg.com).

Made in Japan: Akio Morita and Sony (Paperback) by Akio Morita, Edwin M. Reingold, and Mitsuko Shimomura, Signet (1988).

Management by Objectives

Management by Objectives (MBO) is a method used by management to define objectives for each employee in an organization and then compare their performance against those objectives. Ideally the goals of each individual are aligned with those of the entire organization and will be designed with a great deal of input from the individual both in terms of setting the targets and tracking performance against the objectives. Although known primarily a tool of business, MBO is also used in government, most notably by President Nixon in 1973 with his Management by Objectives initiative that asked each department head to seek a sharper focus on results.

The individual's objectives are tied to the broader organization's objectives so that if done correctly, achieving individual objectives will contribute to the organization achieving its business objectives. Ideally, management and employees buy into the objectives and understand how their individual objectives are tied into the broader organizational objectives. Ultimately it is thought that employees will take greater responsibility for achieving their own objectives if they can observe and understand a direct link to the objectives of their organization. The end goal of using MBO in an organization is to focus on the desired results and attempt to align the results at the business unit level, functional level, and individual level with the desired business results.

MBO was first popularized as a business concept by Peter Drucker in 1954 in his book *The Practice of Management*. According to Drucker, managers today often get so absorbed with day to day activities and tasks that they overlook how their work contributes to the mission or purpose of the broader organization. By implementing MBO, organizations can help their managers and individual employees to reconnect with the central purpose of their organization. A number of important principles of MBO as described by Drucker are the cascading of organizational goals and objectives, identification of specific objectives for each individual, participative decision making, explicit timeframe for delivering results, and performance evaluation and feedback to close the loop.

The MBO method also introduced the SMART—specific, measurable, achievable, realistic and time related—criteria for setting objectives so that users of the process set targets that can be measured and tracked.

In practice MBO usually involves implementation of a four step process:

Why I Do This: Clinical Educator, Critical Care Services
Marie Connolly, RN, CCRN

My family was stunned when, at eighteen, I proudly announced my intention to making nursing my career. After all, I was the "sensitive one," who was afraid of old people when I was young. I was the child who fainted every time a kid in the class got sick to their stomach. I wasn't too sure I would be able to make a difference as a nurse myself, but something inside made me feel that it was the right choice for me.

That was twenty-nine years ago. I have been working and loving my job ever since. The difference between medicine and nursing is, at least to me, that medicine treats the diseases, and nursing treats the human beings afflicted with those diseases. Nursing balances the science of the profession and the art of caring in a complete and whole feeling of satisfaction. You are a medical professional, a teacher, an advocate, a psychologist, and a human touch for your patients when you are a nurse.

My first love in nursing was in intensive care, and I have been in that field most of my years. My subspecialty is cardiology and cardiovascular surgery. However, I've had so many experiences, from delivering babies to holding someone's hand as they die. I've been a caring participant in some of life's most painful and tragic moments, and have been lucky enough to see some true miracles.

My job right now is to help other nurses and teach them to be specialists in cardiac and critical care. I plan new therapies and processes to continually improve the ways we care for patients and families. And, at least once or twice a day, I stop in to a patient's room to see how they are, and spend a few minutes with them, perhaps answering questions they may have about their conditions. To me, there is nothing better than being at the bedside with a patient who needs care, whether physical or emotional, just to make things a little bit better.

One of the biggest benefits of this career is the ability to learn and grow, and to change your specialty, if you choose to, many times before your career is at an end. You will never have to search for work, for the entire world is in need of skilled and caring nurses in all fields of practice.

You can make a small difference at a very big moment, or a big difference in a small one—either way, you make a difference.

And that's why I do what I do.

organizational objective setting, manager objective setting, individual objective setting, and objective review.

Organizational Objective Setting: The first step requires top management of the enterprise to review and clearly articulate the central purpose of the organization. The top management then sets objectives for the organization that will provide direction to the entire organization.

Manager Objective Setting: Using the organization's objectives as a starting point, senior managers throughout the organization develop the objectives of their business units or divisions. These business unit objectives should be clearly articulated such that the members of that unit understand how achieving their unit's objectives will contribute to the objectives of the broader organization or business.

Individual Objective Setting: Based on the objectives for his or her organizational unit, each employee works with his or her manager to set individual objectives which once again must meet the SMART criteria.

Objective Review: After objectives have been set at every level of the organization from top management down to the first line supervisors and each individual employee of an organization, the organization is prepared to implement a management by objective system. This requires each manager and each of his or her employees review the objectives set out at the start and identify where progress has been made and where there continue to be opportunities to improve against the objectives. In many organizations that use Management by Objective as a performance improvement tool as well as a tool to deliver results, there will be an interim review that is intended to help the individual reach the desired results with the benefit of mid-term feedback and coaching.

In addition to the proliferation of MBO systems in the corporate world, this system of management has also been implemented in several of the military agencies in the United States in an attempt to address the perceived inefficiencies in those organizations. While the branches of the military in the United States are known for their authoritarian form of management—as opposed to participatory management styles—supporters of using MBO in the military argue that the MBO method can be implemented in this type of organization when military managers are trained to adapt their management styles to fit the situation they are managing. A further challenge of implementing MBO in non-business organizations is the nature of the results expected. Unlike corporate situations, military and other government situations may not have the same financial results as the driver of their system. Obviously in this situation, the results orientation will require some additional efforts to identify appropriate quantifiable and measurable results or targets.

Critics of MBO practices argue that is it much too easy for managers to fail to outline, and agree with their employees, what it is that everyone is trying to achieve. MBO requires carefully written descriptions of the objectives and a timeline for monitoring and achieving those results. It also requires that managers are skilled at performance management discussions and familiar with the best way to share feedback with their employees. The process, if done well, requires that managers and their staff agree to what is expected, over what period of time, and with what potential benefits to the organization and to the individual employee.

For example, in a sales organization, the manager and the employee will likely agree on a specific level of change in revenue, pipeline activity, or lead generation. In a call center, the manager and the employee may identify an increase in call volume over a period of time or successful resolution of customer service inquiries. In production, the objectives will likely involve improved efficiency and/or cycle time or output. In all cases, it is important to identify the timeframe during which the improvements are expected and to set very specific and measurable targets.

Other critics of MBO practices argue that this system triggers unethical behaviors from employees who may be tempted to distort financials or other data to achieve their targets.

See also: Drucker, Peter

Further Reading

Beyond Management Objectives: A Management Classic, by Joe D. Batten, Resource Publications, December (2003).

What Management Is: How it Works and Why It's Everyone's Business, by Joan Magretta and Nan Stone, Free Press (April 2002).

Managerial Grid

The Managerial Grid is a behavioral management model. It was introduced by Robert Blake and Jane Mouton in 1964, and identifies five different styles of leadership based on concern for people or relationships and concern for production or task. This model of management style attempts to identify a path, for each manager, to the ideal management or leadership style based on that manager's starting point and attributes. Blake and Mouton later set up a company called Scientific Methods, Inc. to share their concepts of organizational development and management effectiveness more broadly in the corporate world.

The Managerial Grid is composed of two axes: "concern for people/relationship" which is plotted on the vertical axis and "concern for task/production" which is plotted along the horizontal axis. Concern for people and relationships is the degree to which the manager or leader considers the needs of the team member and their areas of personal and professional development when deciding how to achieve the desired results or accomplish a given task. Concern for task or production is the degree to which a manager or leader emphasizes the results, objectives, or organizational efficiency when he or she decides how to accomplish a task or achieve the desired business results.

Supporters of this model of leadership behavior argue that it is appealing because of the simplicity of using two dimensions to describe managerial or leadership behavior. Critics argue that because of the simplicity of the model, the managerial grid can not effectively be used to categorize or develop managers and leaders.

While many managers score near the middle of the two axes, the authors use the extremes to identify four types of leaders: authoritarian leaders who are high on task and low on people, team leaders who are high on task and high on people, country club leaders who are low on task and high on people, and finally impoverished leaders who are both low on task and on people.

The *authoritarian leader* scores high on the task axis and low on the people or relationship axis. These leaders are very task oriented and considered to be quite hard on their employees or staff. Leaders with this score do not encourage cooperation or collaboration in their work and focus largely on schedules, assigning blame, and on completion of the specific task. Individuals who work for this type of manager find it difficult to contribute or develop professionally.

The *team leader* scores high on the task axis as well as on the relationship or people axis. This type of leader uses the power of positive examples and collaborative work to create an environment where all team members feel their perspective is valued and their input is encouraged. These leaders encourage professional development of the individual team members and the idea that the total is greater than the sum of the parts. They support team development as well as individual development and therefore create and lead very effective and productive teams.

The *country club leader* scores low on task and high on the people axis. This type of leader uses rewards to motivate teams and individuals and is most likely very uncomfortable exercising discipline or coercion to accomplish goals. The country club leader is most fearful of damaging his or her relationship with other members of his or her staff or team.

The *impoverished leader* scores low on both the task and relationship/people axis. This type of leader is often considered to delegate and ignore his or her staff. They are committed to neither the task of the business nor the creation, development, or maintenance of the relationships. This type of leader will often find their teams struggle with achieving results and are frustrated with the dynamics of the team itself.

A fifth style of leadership is often referred to as the *middle of the road leader*. Leaders who score in the middle of the grid on both task and people are considered *middle of the road leaders*. Leaders who score in this range attempt to balance the company goals with those of their staff or team. These leaders are considered to achieve acceptable though usually unremarkable performance.

See also: Executive Coach

Further Reading

The New Managerial Grid, by Robert R. Blake and Jane S. Mouton, Jaico Publishing House, New Ed ed. (April 2005).

Signs of Changing Culture:
"Dude, You Need a CEO": The Return of Michael Dell

Published: February 7, 2007 in Knowledge@Wharton

Reproduced with permission from Knowledge@Wharton (http://knowledge.wharton.upenn.edu), the online research and business analysis journal of the Wharton School of the University of Pennsylvania.

It's a common occurrence in Corporate America: An entrepreneurial founder starts a successful business, builds it to a certain size and hands it over to a CEO to run. But then, when things don't go well, the founder steps back in to take direct control of the organization. That, essentially, is what happened last week when Michael Dell returned to become the CEO of Dell, replacing Kevin Rollins. What will it take to turn Dell around? Wharton management professor Peter Cappelli is the director of the school's Center for Human Resources. He spoke with Knowledge@Wharton about these issues.

Knowledge@Wharton: Let me start out by asking you a question about a founder coming back to take the CEO job at a company as Michael Dell did. What is the track record of success in such cases?

Cappelli: I think the record is mixed. And I think that it probably helps to step back a little and ask ourselves something about the context of this. Generally, there's a sense that organizations need different skills at different times. And so, the people who have founded organizations and have the entrepreneurial zeal and the ideas and such often aren't the people who can take the organization to the next phase.

Sometimes you need more administrative skills, more management skills. Sometimes leadership and zeal isn't enough. On the other hand, the founders have a symbolism that becomes very important when they step back in—in terms of the sense that they give the employees or their ability to sell ideas to the outside audience at different points in time.

I think this is really the punch line: Organizations need different things, and you could imagine them changing leaders as a way to try to make that happen.

Knowledge@Wharton: One of the first things that Dell had done after taking charge [again] was to send out this memo that we just heard about, saying that there would be no bonuses for 2006. He described the year as one in which there had been great efforts, but not great results. Do you think that doing away with bonuses is a good idea?

Cappelli: Well, I think that with all management changes like this, there is the distinction between the symbolism and the substance. With respect to this particular case, the end of bonuses—particularly articulated by not only the founder, but the guy who has the biggest financial stake in the company—is really kind of a powerful message.

And, it's a powerful message that comes from the owners . . . that something has got to change. So it certainly is on the symbolism ground, an important statement to shake people up. I think it's also a statement to the investment community and to outsiders, too, that we're taking this seriously. Does it de-motivate people? Yes. Are there some down sides to that? The answer is yes, probably.

I think one of the questions you ask yourself is: What is the purpose of this? And I think a lot of the purpose is the symbolism and the messages to not just insiders, but to outsiders.

Knowledge@Wharton: Another key point in Dell's memo was his attack on bureaucracy, which he says has slowed down the company. Is this surprising for a company that built its reputation on the speed with which its supply chain could make customized computers for customers? And, how does bureaucracy creep into an entrepreneurial organization?

Cappelli: Well, maybe I'll just take a step back on this question and make what may be sort of an unusual observation. I think to a large extent these companies don't know what they're doing. They don't know what they're doing in the sense that they are facing different environments and they need to respond to them and they're not sure how. So in this case, for example, Dell was the darling of many people in the business world because they had this model that seemed to work just incredibly well, and lots of people were copying it, and then the environment changed. It's not that they got bad at executing their model. At least I don't think that's the complaint. It is that the environment changed. They got different competitors who came in with different ideas and the playing field changed.

Now the question is, how do you respond to that? I was looking over the press releases and the analysts' comments on the transition at Dell. They almost all universally praise the idea that Michael Dell is coming back. They almost all universally have nothing to say about what it is that he'll actually do. Some of them are honest enough to say, "Well, the problems don't change with him coming back" and "it's not clear what he's going to do."

The other thing that I thought was interesting about that comment from Dell is that one of the things that Kevin Rollins was seen as good at, was being particularly tough, particularly cost focused—which is exactly what a lot of the analysts say Dell has to do to go forward. In fact, he seemed to be pretty good at the kinds of things that most of the analysts say they ought to be doing.

I think this suggests something general about what's going on in the business world now with leadership ranks—that leaders are a substitute for strategy. Companies really rarely have a clear sense about the direction that they need to go in when something like this happens—that is, the environment around them changes. They substitute new leadership for new strategy.

Whenever there is a change in the direction of a company, it always involves new leaders. I think that this is partly a signal to the investment community, frankly, that they're going to do something different, but what it is, we don't know yet. I think as a result the leadership gets churned much more often than it would have in generations previous, and much more often than it actually deserves to be churned.

As far as I can tell, what Dell says it wants to do [is] exactly the kind of stuff that Kevin Rollins was good at. And it just wasn't working well enough. Changing leadership is just a signal to the business community that "we're taking this seriously and we're going to try something maybe even a little different going forward."

Knowledge@Wharton: Speaking of Kevin Rollins, what do you think was his biggest mistake? Or, is he just a victim of the company needing to send a signal to the investment community that a change is in the offing?

Cappelli: I don't see that he made any obvious mistakes. I met him a few years ago. He seems to be a very articulate guy, a good spokesperson for the company, and apparently he was focused on the kinds of things that the company always saw as their strengths and competitive advantage.

Now, you hear things about his management style—that he was overbearing, or too tough a taskmaster, and all that sort of stuff. Of course, that's exactly what the analysts are saying the company needs now, right? I think he was in the wrong place at the wrong time, and I think that happens to a lot of executives now. And, I think it's more a function of the way business works now.

Knowledge@Wharton: Will this move make it harder for Dell to start grooming a successor—given what happened to Rollins, and the fact that Michael Dell himself was only forty-one and could always step back in and take the reigns again?

Cappelli: Well, I think the answer to the second point—that it's hard to put somebody in this job because the founder is always breathing over your shoulder—there's probably something to that, although it's true in any organization. The average life of a CEO now is about 3 years or so. Any time a company gets in trouble now, the CEO gets dumped. So, I don't think anybody [probably] is going into these jobs with a sense that they're necessarily going to have a long run. And, I think that this is maybe a big problem for U.S. corporations. They are so focused, even the leadership of the companies, on short-term performance that the CEO's recognize that if things go bad in the company, they're going to get tossed out—it makes their focus on short-term performance even stronger. I think, frankly, companies aren't thinking about grooming successors these days, anyway. They talk about it sometimes. They may for a while have somebody in the pipeline who looks like a successor. But then the environment changes and that guy's kicked out, and somebody new is brought in from the outside. You know the talk and the reality are so different on these things, that at some point the talk doesn't even make sense.

Knowledge@Wharton: Before it got into its recent troubles, Dell seemed to be highly successful in the PC business, but less so in other consumer electronics products. Are there any lessons here for companies that don't stick to their knitting?

Cappelli: Well, I suppose that certainly is the one lesson that people would begin to point to, and that is to stick to what you're good at. Dell's computer market was good not just because of its marketing, but because of the way it was able to assemble the computers in the first place, the modular assembly processes that lay behind that. I guess the extent to which you can keep the whole model together is crucial—that it's not just the way you sell things, but it's the way you build them and all of these things fit together. And, if you start branching out away from that, you could have some problems.

Knowledge@Wharton: In contrast to Dell, Apple's had tremendous success with its foray into consumer electronics with the iPod, and it wants to build further on that success with the iPhone. Are there any lessons that Dell could learn from Apple?

Cappelli: Well, we have some ideas about why Apple has worked well. Apple is a company that is making its money in a completely different way. Apple is making its money by innovation. Dell was making its money by selling the same stuff, more or less, that everybody else was selling, selling it cheaper, and selling it in a customized way.

You could see why the return of the founder at Apple might be a bigger deal than the return of the founder at Dell. Apple is a company that is really trying to go directly to the consumer and persuade them that something is new and novel. And you bring back the founder, who was famous for doing something new and novel. Maybe it helped energize Apple to do this, but it certainly helped to sell it.

At Dell, it's not so obvious that they've got the same market and the same problem and that the same solution would work there. So, I think the short answer is that there are not a lot of lessons [really] for Dell from Apple. I think that this is probably also something that we should just confess to: In this modern business environment, where things are changing so quickly, strategies are so ad-hoc and so volatile.

Companies really don't have good ideas about what they're doing. They're changing all the time in response to the business environment. We don't mean to suggest this is because they are not smart enough or not capable enough. It's just an incredibly hard problem they've got—not just to make money, but to figure out how to make money when the markets are changing or your competitors are changing around you, and new products come in all of a sudden that you didn't anticipate.

And how you respond to this is very tricky. [Companies] really don't know; they are fishing and it's understandable why they are fishing. But I think the big lesson from this Dell experience is that when companies get into trouble, they change their executives, whether it makes sense in terms of a new direction or not. They change their executives because people expect that a changed executive will mean a change in policy. Maybe it's easier to change policy with a new executive, too. That might be true. But I think a lot of this is symbolism. And it's not because the company has got a clear, new agenda, a new direction, and they necessarily need different people with different competencies to do it, and that they know how to put all of that stuff together.

Knowledge@Wharton: One last question: If Michael Dell was sitting in this room with us right now, what advice would you give him?

Cappelli: I'm not sure that we have any clear advice to give him. I think that it would be interesting to hear how he's thinking about the problem. And I think the very best thing that one could hope, that executives do in situations like this, is to think carefully and objectively about what the problem is, what their capabilities are and how they can respond to these situations.

The quality of thinking is probably the best that you can hope for in these contexts. The other thing that you can probably be sure of is that, in a year or two, whatever they thought today is going to be irrelevant and they'll be on to something else.

Mass Customization

Mass customization means making and selling—or going to market with—mass-produced goods that are tailored or tweaked somehow to meet the needs or desires of individual customers. The process is widely considered to combine the best of "custom made" and "mass produced" goods.

Mass production is the production of large quantities of low cost products or services. Custom-made products or services generally cost more to produce, and can therefore demand a price premium over mass-produced products or services. Historically, mass produced products were not tailored for individual tastes or needs. Consumers were willing to purchase products that weren't exactly what they wanted because those "mass produced" goods were less expensive than custom-made alternatives. Traditionally, companies have assumed that trade offs between high quality and low cost or production efficiency and customization are required decisions they must make for their business.

Mass customization seeks the elusive middle ground. The idea is that by using leading edge production processes, tools, or methods, a company can produce customized products and/or services at more affordable and competitive prices. In essence, mass customization is considered the frontier in delivering products to a target market of one customer. Mass customization, in marketing, manufacturing, or management, uses much more flexible computer assisted production systems to produce the custom output but at a fraction of the cost of traditional manufacturing. The critical element is the ability to provide flexibility of individual customization.

Dell is perhaps one of the most well known examples of a company that provides mass customization of its products. Dell calls their innovative approach "build to order." Each computer that leaves a Dell warehouse has been configured to the particular customer's specifications. In essence, each Dell product is made to order which traditionally would have involved much higher production costs. Dell has been able to deliver mass customization by implementing an order entry system that requires relatively little or no involvement by Dell employees in the order entry and product specification process. By reducing order entry and sales costs, Dell is able to produce custom products at much lower cost and can pass along the savings to their customers. The result is to give each customer what he or she wants at a cost that traditionally would have been associated only with mass production.

Other examples of successful mass customization include some cosmetic companies that create unique mixes of their product to provide custom cosmetics and a number of clothing manufacturers where you can have custom jeans or blouses produced to your exact specifications.

The automobile industry has struggled with the potential for mass customization for decades. At this point consumers can specify some components on their automobiles but only very high end vehicles would be considered truly customized and therefore do not fit the definition of mass customization. Essentially, the automobile industry has settled for offering various configurations on mass produced products while at times hoping to convince consumers that they have more input on the actual design of their vehicles.

In mass customization, customers are integrated into the value creation process. They define, configure, or modify a company's "solution" (product or offering) to fit their needs. Customization demands that the customer share his or her product or service needs into the design specification process. Mass customization is a product or service differentiation strategy for a company, in other words, but it involves the customer in the design of their product in some way.

Companies that embrace mass customization are often targeting customers who were previously purchasing mass produced products. While these customers are often willing to pay some premium for the customization of their products, customers are not usually willing to pay the full premium of customized products. The advantage of mass customization is that the product is customized to the needs of the individual customer but both the company and the customer share some of the cost savings of using more innovative technologies of mass customized products. Another advantage: the product is usually "demanded" before it is created. So companies have a built-in system that can guide their rate of production.

See also: Just-in-Time

Further Reading

Markets of One: Creating Customer-Unique Value through Mass Customization, by James H. Gilmore and B. Joseph Pine (eds.), Harvard Business School Press (February 2000)

Mass Customization: The New Frontier in Business Competition (paperback), by B. Joseph Pine and Stan Davis, Harvard Business School Press, New Ed ed. (April 1999)

Matrix Organizations

Matrix organizations are companies in which people are organized by function (the type of job they perform, such as accounting) but also by project (what they're working on and where in the company that work fits at a given time).

In the 1970s and 1980s, the business environment became far more complex, due to several factors: the globalization of markets, new technologies, faster product life cycles, and even more intense competition. While these factors demanded faster and more complex solutions and strategies, many corporations realized that, internally, they were organized in a way that actually hindered their ability to respond.

Traditionally, most companies were organized into one of two types of structures: top-down hierarchies or project/product-focused organizations.

- Top-down hierarchies, also known as functional organizations. In this type of structure, the CEO provides overall direction, while the managers of each major function (marketing, sales, finance, etc.) report to him/her. The employees in each major function report to its manager.

  The same structure exists within each "function" or discipline. For example, in a marketing department, the managers of each marketing function (sales, advertising, public relations, marketing research, etc.) report to the head of the marketing department.

  Although organization charts for this type of structure are typically drawn in a hierarchical pyramid design, no company operates in quite such a stringent and restricted manner. The line of authority from the CEO down makes clear to all employees the company's philosophy, policies, business objectives, etc.

- At the other end of the continuum is the project, or product-focused organization. In this type of structure, a multi-disciplinary team is formed, mirroring the functional structure but organized under a project manager. These teams are focused on a specific project or product launch, and are often temporary in nature.

A matrix organization was derived as a combination of both forms of organizations, in an effort to maintain the advantages of each. Although both project and matrix structures are cross-functional, there are key differences. Project organizations are focused around specific and finite projects, while matrix organizations deal with ongoing management issues.

In a matrix, an employee has a dual reporting relationship, one functional and one operational. For example, an accountant's functional manager may be the chief financial officer, but his/her project manager is the team leader. The functional reporting relationship is generally the stronger of the two relationships, since the functional manager performs the employee's performance evaluation, and determines the employee's compensation. Needless to say, this can put the employee in a difficult position; they may receive conflicting direction from their bosses. For this to work, communication between managers is critical. Matrix organizations are quite common in the case of a headquarters and branch offices, nationally or internationally. An IT specialist in the London office may report functionally to the chief technology officer at headquarters in New York, but also reports operationally to the London Regional Manager.

Matrix organizations are by nature complex, and the approach offers some clear pros and cons. Supporters of matrix management, for their part, tend to stress that, with the matrix approach:

- There is greater sharing of information across functions,
- This type of structure does not require as many layers of management as a functional organization,
- Greater flexibility of staffing. A manager can "loan" an employee, knowing that change is not permanent,
- Improved professional development for employees, who are not "siloed" within their function. Instead, they are exposed to other disciplines, and can more easily view the big picture.

While those who don't prefer a matrix approach note that:

- The dual reporting relationship can be confusing to employees and result in divided loyalties,
- The success of this management structure is contingent upon the cooperation and close working relationship of the functional and operational managers,
- The two managers may have different goals, objectives, and priorities, and there may be differences concerning the allocation of resources,
- Overlapping responsibilities could lead to turf battles.

The challenges of working in a matrix organization are magnified as a company grows. Small companies, especially start-ups often find themselves operating to some extent in an essentially matrix organization—with smaller numbers people are more likely to know and trust each other, and share staff and information to get the job done. As organizations grow and relationships become more distant, and at times even competitive, the matrix organization becomes more strained. Often the impact of the strain is most evident in middle management who is caught having to report to two bosses with competing objectives. For example, in meeting the needs of the functional boss they will fail to meet the assignments of the operational boss. Faced with such a "no-win" scenario they will often make an informal decision about "who is my real boss" (i.e., the one that impacts compensation or advancement the most) and work to meet that person's objectives. Other scenarios arise even when the two bosses in a matrix organization are aligned in terms of goals and objectives. Often the result is the volume of work—essentially doing the work of multiple people in a single role. When the strain of matrix management becomes evident, employees have become known to feel "lost in the matrix," alluding to the 1999 movie when the central character faces two levels of reality—the everyday existence and a more significant underlying reality.

See also: Learning Organization

Further Reading

The Matrix Organization Reloaded: Adventures in Team and Project Management (Creating Corporate Cultures), by Marvin R. Gottlieb, Praeger Publishers (August 2007).

Megatrends

Megatrend is the term most commonly used to indicate a widespread trend or major impact or in other words those trends that would widely be considered to be "larger than life." A megatrend is a large scale change, often social, economic, political, environmental, or technological change or phenomenon that emerges slowly but likely to have long-term staying power and the ability to have widespread impact for a long period of time. In most instances, a megatrend will impact more than one country and may in fact have consequences on a global scale. Megatrends typically include several sub trends that will have significant impact in and of themselves and when combined have a far greater impact than the sub trends themselves. Examples of megatrends include global warming or global climate change, aging population, bioengineering, spirituality, and population growth. Businesses that are able to capitalize on a megatrend, by offering products or services that tap into the far-reaching influence of a trend often experience a period of growth and success.

One of the more talked about and perhaps controversial megatrends, global climate change, is described by former Presidential candidate Al Gore in his 2005 documentary movie entitled *An Inconvenient Truth*. This megatrend includes the sub trends of sea level rise, decrease in ozone, and atmospheric warming, all of which will have significant impact on a global level.

In the case of aging population, the sub trends include buying habits, elder care, health care, and issues related to retirement. The aging population impacts individuals, government agencies, health care agencies, the health care system, as well as the hiring and benefits functions in corporations around the globe.

Bioengineering as a megatrend includes sub trends such as stem cell research, genetic engineering, DNA research, and cloning issues. This megatrend has already had significant impact on industry as well as government policies around the world.

In business culture, the term megatrend was first coined by John Naisbitt who identifies himself as a futurist, in his 1982 book entitled *Megatrends: Ten New Directions Transforming Our Lives*. While Naisbitt's work was considered by many critics to have a largely United States orientation and therefore not entirely fitting the more far reaching and global orientation of the term megatrend, Naisbitt did identify a number of important megatrends that have had significant impact on the global community in the past two decades. In 1990 Naisbitt co-authored another book with his then wife, Patricia Aburdene entitled *Megatrends 2000: Ten New Directions for the 1990s*. Some of the megatrends that Aburdene and Naisbitt successfully predicted include: the emergence of the information society, the development of a global economy, hierarchies moving to networking, and the global economic boom of the 1990s. In 2005, Aburdene published a third book *Megatrends 2010: The Rise of Conscious Capitalism* which focuses more on what she refers to as the spiritual evolution of business including the sub trends of value-driven consumers, socially responsible investment, and a new model of corporate leadership that does not look or behave like the traditional authoritarian and highly compensated model of management.

The term megatrend also has been used by many organizations in the name of their company or organizations to draw attention to their products, services, and mission. One example, American Megatrends Incorporated (AMI), based in the United States develops PC based hardware that the company claims is often leading edge product such as motherboards based on Intel's 386 and 486 processor platforms, first to support USB, and the first to create BUI BIOS interface with mouse support.

While Naisbitt and Aburdene are the most popularly noted authors on the subject of megatrends and have expanded their predictions to global issues and issues of social justice, many other authors and experts compile lists each year or decade on what they predict will be the megatrends of the next century. These individuals, knowns as "futurists" highlight the trends (though often not megatrends) that will impact business and the world.

See also: Innovation

Further Reading

Megatrends 2010: The Rise of Conscious Capitalism, by Patricia Aburdene, Hampton Roads Publishing Company, New Ed ed. (May 2007).

Mid-Career

Mid-career may be thought of as the professional equivalent of the mid-life crisis and refers to the period of time in an individual's professional life when they are not yet ready or able to retire and yet clearly no longer a novice or young professional starting out in the work force. For some individuals who have been in one profession or even employed by the same company for a long period of time, mid-career is often defined as that period of time when they evaluate their past and consider what they most want to do with their future. For some, this involves self evaluation and potentially a career shift to work that is more fulfilling or for which they have greater passion. For others, mid-career signals a desire to work less and spend more time on leisure activities. And yet for others, particularly women reentering the workforce after their children have grown, mid-career is a new professional beginning. For a final group, those who have been out-placed, fired, or made redundant by their employers, mid-career is a personal and professional crisis for which they were largely or entirely unprepared.

Mid-career issues affect professionals and individuals in just about every industry segment. Medicine, law, business, government, the ministry, and academia have each confronted issues of mid-career burn out or skill loss among workers. Blue collar workers also experience mid-career issues but the majority of research and interest has been focused on the mid-career issues affecting white collar workers or professionals.

Many professionals experience a growing sense of uneasiness in their 40s and 50s that the work they are doing was not what they intended to do with the rest of their lives or they thought what they were doing was their life work but find they are no longer satisfied with the work they are doing. Professionals who have lost the enthusiasm they once had for their work often share the following traits: their work has little connection to those things that they truly care about, they are often good at their work but not fulfilled by it, and they tend to work towards short term results rather than long term goals. Many in this group find that their definition of success has changed from job title, level of expertise, and/or financial security to definitions of success that involve personal achievements and relationships with others or with their community.

Other mid-career business people have become alienated from their work in large companies and look to establish themselves either as entrepreneurs or executives in smaller companies where they believe that can have a more direct impact on the business—an opportunity for once to be the one to call the shots and make the rules. While many such mid-career transitions are successful, some fail. One counselor in such transitions has identified issues in mid-career executive transitions from the big pond to the small pond. They include: being all things to all people (without the support personnel they can delegate to), constant distractions from small problems, a loss of influence and prestige, and a loss of control over their time.

Professional who have been made redundant or been fired from their jobs have an increasing set of resources available to help them find their next position. Some employers provide a range of services for their former employees including outplacement employment counseling, use of temporary office space, and extended benefits plans.

For some individuals, mid-career evaluation and planning is triggered by a crisis, either personal or professional in nature. For others, mid-career evaluation is part of their personal or professional development journey. An entire industry has also grown up around the need for services targeted at mid-career professionals. Some firms specialize in coaching to help mid-career professionals consider what options are appealing both inside and outside their current organization. Other firms specialize in working with companies that wish to support their former employees while other firms specialize in working with individuals.

Several educational institutions have established programs specifically targeted at mid-career professionals and some such as Harvard Business School have created programs specifically targeted at the women alumni who are reentering the workforce after a number of years away for personal or family leave. The media has also highlighted a number of well known business executives who have left a successful career at mid-career in pursuit of a new career in politics, nonprofits, or other social enterprise organizations. Notably, a number of successful and high profile executives have moved into more advisory roles with their current organizations to pursue more philanthropic goals making use of their own high profile status.

For example, by July 2008, Bill Gates has committed to moving out of his professional role and focusing on the Bill and Melinda Gates Foundation where he believes he can have a greater impact by donating some of his personal resources and expertise to worthy global causes. One of the former presidents of the United States, Ronald Reagan, was originally a movie actor and later turned to politics. And a large number of movie and TV actors have contributed significantly to global issues while remaining involved in their film careers. George Clooney has received attention recently for his work in Darfur while Angelina Jolie has traveled the globe to advance issues of social justice. Yet for ordinary people opting for a mid-career change, especially in change from the for-profit to the not-for-profit sectors, there can be significant consequences. For example, a sales executive in a technology firm saw her income fall from $200,000 to $40,000 when she began teaching in a public school. Although happy with her mid-career choice and the fulfillment it brought, there were substantive lifestyle changes that accompanied it.

The idea of finding oneself at "mid-career" invites a host of questions and decisions. It can be a source of angst; it can be a time when people begin to contemplate their legacies. It can also be source of inspiration, and motivation to make the next steps as meaningful as possible.

See also: Lifetime Employment; War for Talent

Further Reading

The Mid-Career Success Guide: Planning for the Second Half of Your Working Life,
    by Sally J. Power, Praeger Publishers (2006).
"Navigating Through a Mid-Career Crisis," located on www.allbusiness.com.
www.humanresources.about.com

Mission Statement

A mission statement defines a company's fundamental goals and is a key
component in the development of an organization's corporate culture. A
meaningful mission statement can get employees to take their jobs to
heart, to care about their company, and to align their actions with the core
goals of the corporation. Some companies have a singular mission statement, while others combine a mission statement with corporate values.

Some companies' mission statements reflect the founder's core values
and beliefs. Others are less personality driven and describe the mission
more in terms of strategy and outcome. Generally speaking though, an
effective mission statement has four components: purpose for the company, a strategy, a set of values, and standards and behaviors. Unless an
expression from the founders, defining a mission statement is a significant
task involving many levels of people in an organization. The process generally begins with a senior management team developing and then editing
several versions of the mission statement. When a draft is ready, the company will then solicit input from others in the organization, usually
through focus groups or surveys. Based on that input, the draft is revised
and finalized.

Arguably creating the wording for the mission statement is the easiest
part of the process. To make the mission statement meaningful in the organization it then needs to be communicated and reinforced by management. Scrutiny by employees is high—they want to know that management is willing "to walk the talk of the mission statement," and that this
is not yet another flavor of the month program that will come and go.
Several techniques have been used to inculcate a mission statement into
an organization including face-to-face meetings, town hall sessions where
employees are invited to ask questions, and newsletters that highlight employees that have accomplished a task aligned with the mission statement.
From a structural perspective, companies also review human resources pol-

icies and compensation practices to ensure that they are aligned with the mission statement.

One of the most powerful uses of the mission statement occurred in 1982 after seven people died after taking Tylenol laced with cyanide. Although it was found that the tampering had occurred after the Tylenol had been shipped from the factory, J&J (Johnson & Johnson) issued a nation-wide recall for its most profitable product and halted associated advertising and promotion. Then CEO James Burke applied his company's mission statement, the J&J Credo, to every component of the situation with special emphasis on the first line, "We believe our first responsibility is to the doctors, nurses, and patients, to mothers and fathers, and all others who use our products and services."

Although the J&J Credo was written by General Robert Wood Johnson fifty years earlier, it stood the company in good stead. As noted in the book *Say It and Live It* (page 37), James Burke was quoted as saying, "After the crisis was over we realized that no meeting had been called to make the first critical decision. Every one of us knew what we had to do. We had the Credo to guide us." With that guide J&J was able to recover—with its market share falling to about 7 percent after the incident, but ultimately rebounding to its 35 percent share.

Following are a few sample mission statements. It is often an interesting exercise to see if the company can be identified through its statement alone.

Ben & Jerry's as seen at: http://www.benjerry.com/our_company/our_mission/index.cfm. Ben & Jerry's is founded on and dedicated to a sustainable corporate concept of linked prosperity.
Our mission consists of three interrelated parts:
Product Mission
   To make, distribute & sell the finest quality all natural ice cream & euphoric concoctions with a continued commitment to incorporating wholesome, natural ingredients and promoting business practices that respect the Earth and the Environment.
Economic Mission
   To operate the Company on a sustainable financial basis of profitable growth, increasing value for our stakeholders & expanding opportunities for development and career growth for our employees.

Social Mission

To operate the company in a way that actively recognizes the central role that business plays in society by initiating innovative ways to improve the quality of life locally, nationally & internationally.

Intel as seen at: http://www.intel.com/intel/company/corp1.htm

Intel's mission statement, values, and objectives

Our mission

Delight our customers, employees, and shareholders by relentlessly delivering the platform and technology advancements that become essential to the way we work and live.

Our values

Customer orientation

Results orientation

Risk taking

Great place to work

Quality

Discipline

Our objectives

Extend leadership in silicon and platform manufacturing

Deliver architectural innovation for market-driving platforms

Drive worldwide growth

Mission statements can be powerful sources of motivation and focus in times of crisis. They can also provide strong day-to-day guidance at the broadest levels. Most mission statements likely do not live up to this promise. But the potential is what keeps companies honing their statements, and ensuring that employees understand and engage with them.

See also: Code of Ethics; Competitive Advantage; Value Proposition

Further Reading

For a humorous take on mission statements: http://www.dilbert.com/comics/dilbert/games/career/bin/ms.cgi.

How to Write a Mission Statement, by Janel M. Radtke, published 1998, located at www.tgci.com/magazine.

www.businessplans.org (Business Resource Software, Inc., Center for Business Planning)

Moments of Truth

In 1986, Jan Carlzon, the former president of Scandinavian Airlines, wrote a book, *Moments of Truth*, chronicling his leadership of the airline during a turnaround. His management philosophy was defined around what he called "moments of truth," which are opportunities when employees of an organization interface with those outside the organization (primarily customers). The interaction at these moments defines the organization's ability to live up to its promise, especially when something has gone wrong. In his book, Carlzon defined the moment of truth in business as this: "Anytime a customer comes into contact with any aspect of a business, however remote, is an opportunity to form an impression."

At SAS, Carlzon focused on the frequent business traveler and using the "moment of truth" methodology analyzed the airlines' operation to ensure that it was attuned to that market. For example, Carlzon noted, "We decided to stop regarding expenses as an evil that we should minimize and to begin looking at them as resources for improving our competitiveness. Expenses, could, in fact give us a competitive edge, if they contributed to our goal of serving the business customer . . . We decided to be one percent better at 100 things instead of 100 percent better at one thing" (*Moments of Truth*, p. 24).

While the business world was impressed with Carlzon's leadership of SAS, it was captivated by the notion of moments of truth and with it the ability to improve customer service. As the U.S. economy was moving toward service industries, the concept had particular resonance. In his book Carlzon highlighted moments of truth in the airline business: when a reservation is made, when bags are checked, when the customer obtains his/her boarding pass, when they are at the gate, how they are treated by flight attendants during the flight, and how they are greeted at the destination, etc.

Yet every business can define its own moments of truth and those moments of truth change as the industry changes. Consider retail banking. Several years ago, the customer went to the bank during the restrictive hours of 10 A.M. to 3 P.M. They waited in line to see a teller to transact their business. Today, most of retail banking in done at automated teller machines for routine transactions—hence the moments of truth have changed from the politeness and knowledge of the teller to the accuracy and maintenance of the ATM network and the fees charged. Yet the concept of delivery during a moment of truth continues. A McKinsey study

Why I Do This: Commercial Airline Pilot
Eric McIntosh

I'm a pilot for a major airline. I fly a 767 internationally, from New York's Kennedy Airport to locations throughout Europe and Western Asia, including Moscow and Bombay.

Pilots are often away from home a lot—but in this job, you do have a lot of control over how much you do. Basically, as a commercial pilot, you work hourly. That is, you get paid by the hour. I get paid from the time the airplane leaves the gate, to the time it pulls into the gate at the destination. But you do have a lot of control over how much you work. For example, a typical month for me would include maybe four trips, with each trip lasting three or four days. Flying out, staying at the destination overnight, flying back. I generally work an average of fourteen days per month—less in the summer, more in the winter.

I suspect that for a lot of people, becoming a pilot is something you think about fairly early on. I knew from the time I was twelve years old that I wanted to be a pilot. An airline pilot came into my school for a career day, and I was hooked. My dad had been a military pilot, as well, and even though he had retired when I was very young, I knew that he had enjoyed flying.

There are a lot of hurdles to clear, if you want to become a pilot. First you need a four-year college degree; the airlines tend to prefer science and engineering degrees. Then once you have your degree, you can either get your training through the military, or on your own. I flew for the United States Air Force for eight and a half years, where I received all my training. The civilian route is very expensive; it's a huge investment, by the time you get all of the certifications and licenses required. When you go civilian, you also have to start working for smaller, regional airlines, where the pay is lower and the hours are longer.

There are a lot of great things about my job. I enjoy the challenge of flying a big airplane and all the responsibility associated with that. I enjoy the fact that it is very task oriented; I also enjoy that the job is a big challenge during the flight, but that as soon as the flight is over, you're done. You hang your hat at work. When you're not working, you're not working.

You might like this kind of job if you enjoy a lot of responsibility and a high degree of challenge. Every time I fly, the job is a little bit different. You might also enjoy this kind of job if you like being your own boss. I work for a huge organization, but the organizational tree doesn't seem to apply directly. No one really second guesses you; you are making the decisions. You feel as if you're your own boss, even though technically you're not.

Loving travel is also a piece of it. I didn't get into this job because of the travel per se. But the travel in and of itself is very interesting; you do spend a few days in lots of different locations; you get twenty-four hours in these spots, and you do get to see the world, albeit one day at a time. Of course, I also hate being away from my family. That's one of the downsides of the job. That, and dealing with jetlag. But when you're gone 15 days a month, you really enjoy being home when you're home. And when you're home, you're really there, 24/7, for a time. That's a great thing.

("Better Service in Banks," *McKinsey Quarterly*, Issue 1, 2005) that entailed the survey of 2,100 retail banking customers found that customers that had a "negative experience during the previous twenty-four months kept 4 percent less with the bank than those that had a positive experience."

For management then there were three important lessons that evolved from *Moments of Truth*. 1) Understand your target customer. 2) Create not only the products and services that the target desires, but also the business policies and procedures that support service delivery to that customer. 3) Create a system of empowerment that allows for service recovery when the organization fails in a moment of truth. Indeed, the latter point often stays with the customer. For example, most people have had the experience of ordering a meal in a restaurant and it arriving with some flaw. When the restaurant realizes it has fallen short during that moment of truth and attempts to recover by offering a free substitute it will often regain what it lost.

See also: Change Agent/Change Management; Turnaround

Further Reading

"Moments of Truth," in the Sounding Off column in *Sounding Line*, by John Ashenhurst, Editor, located at http://www.soundingline-archives.com/0301_Editorial.htm.
Moments of Truth, by Jan Carlzon, Collins (1989).

Myers-Briggs Type Indicator® (MBTI)

The Myers-Briggs Type Indicator® (MBTI) is a self-administered personality inventory, based on C.G. Jung's work in the 1920s on psychological types. The objective of this inventory is to help people understand their own preferred way of perceiving information and drawing conclusions. It is also used as an aid to understanding how other people perceive information and make judgments.

C.G. Jung's work on personality type was first presented in Germany in 1913. In 1917, Katharine Briggs began her own personality research, and developed a four-type framework.

In 1926, Katharine Briggs published two articles on Jung's theories. Her daughter, Isabel Briggs Myers, built on her mother's research work, and in 1942 the "Briggs-Myers Type Indicator® was created, followed by a handbook in 1944. In 1956, the indicator was officially changed to the Myers-Briggs Type Indicator® (MBTI)."

Detractors of the Indicator note that neither Katharine Briggs nor Isabel Myers had scientific, medical, psychiatric, or psychological qualifications.

The Indicator identifies people's self-reported preferences on four dimensions. It is important to note that each dimension is on a continuum. This typology purports to measure your preferred style along this continuum.

1. **Extraversion/Introversion.** Do you prefer to deal with people, situations, and other "external" things (extraversion), or do you prefer to deal with ideas, beliefs, etc., that make up your "inner world" (introversion)?
2. Sensing/Intuition. Do you prefer to deal with facts, concrete issues, descriptions (sensing), or do you prefer to think about new ideas, possibilities, things less obvious (intuition)?
3. **Thinking/Feeling.** Are you prone to make decisions based on logic, analysis, and objective approaches (thinking), or are your decisions based on personal beliefs and values (feeling)?
4. **Judging/Perceiving.** Do you prefer a highly organized life, based on established ideas, or are you open to new possibilities and less structure?

The assessment instrument is comprised of ninety-three multiple-choice questions. The results of the assessment are categorized into one of sixteen personality "types," based on interaction of the dimensions noted above. Each type has its own specific characteristics, as well as its own acronym, indicating preferences. For example, "ENTJ" refers to "extravert, intuition, thinking, judging." The descriptors of someone within this typology: assumes a leadership role quickly, blunt, decisive; Forceful in presentation of ideas; Quickly sees problems with current procedures and policies; and enjoys developing systems to solve organizational issues as well as long-term planning. An ENTJ is most likely well read, and enjoys both expanding their own knowledge, as well as informing others.

It is important to note what the Indicator does *not* measure: ability, character, mental health. All types are equally desirable; there is no one preferred type. The Indicator is frequently used in a corporate environment, for team building and professional development purposes.

The results of this typology are geared toward helping the individual understand their own preferred thinking and work style, as well as those of colleagues or customers. For example, sales approaches can be tailored according to how the customer prefers to receive information.

The Indicator is not without its detractors. It focuses on how you *prefer* to act, not how you actually do, so its value as an assessment tool has been questioned. Test/retest reliability is apparently low, particularly after some time has passed. But despite its detractors, the Myers-Briggs Type Indicator® has endured, with its sixtieth anniversary in October 2006 and remains one of the most popular and widely administered tools, with about 2.5 million tests conducted annually. As Douglas Shuit noted in *Workforce Management*, in December 2003, "Both critics and supporters say that the Indicator endures because it does a good job of pointing up differences between people, offers individuals a revealing glimpse of themselves, and is a valuable asset in team-building, improving communication, and resolving personality-based conflict."

See also: Emotional Intelligence; Headhunter; The Peter Principle

Further Reading

www.myersbriggs.org

Napster

Napster was a company that existed for only a short time as a source for downloading free music, yet it opened up a Pandora's box of legal and ethical issues regarding how we obtain the music that we listen to.

In the late 1990s the MP3 file format for music files had hit its stride. The MP3 format made song files small enough that they could be moved around the Internet and downloaded to a personal computer quickly enough for the general consumer to use. Originally, websites like MP3 .com provided a location where anyone could upload a song and store it on a central database. Anyone wanting a song on the database had to search for it, find it, and download it. While this worked, it was cumbersome as there wasn't one central location for all of the songs.

In 1999, eighteen-year-old Shawn Fanning was frustrated with not being able to find the MP3 files that he and his friends wanted, and he came up with the idea that if you used a Peer to Peer file sharing system, you could eliminate the central server and bulky search requirements. With the help of some friends and the financial backing of his uncle, Shawn wrote the code to create Napster. With peer-to-peer file sharing you download the actual files right to your computer rather than accessing them on a central server.

In general, Napster worked as follows: Someone who wanted to download a song needed a computer with the Napster program, a directory that had been shared, and a connection to the Internet. They opened their Napster program, typed in the song they wanted, and the system went out over the Internet to search for another computer on the Internet that had the song for which the user was searching. Once found, the song could be downloaded directly to the first user's computer from the other computer, and then played as many times as the user wished.

This was immensely popular especially on college campuses as many colleges and universities were just completing large investments in schoolwide networks so students and faculty would be able to use computers effectively in classes. Combine with that the fact that college students as a whole tend to like music, and don't typically have a lot of money, and you had the perfect scenario for Napster to find a dedicated audience for free music downloading.

As one might expect, the music companies and artists were divided in their response to this idea. Some felt that this was great free advertising, but others thought that it was illegal as royalties were not being paid to the artists and the music companies felt that they were losing sales. The heavy metal band Metallica filed a lawsuit against Napster in 2000 because a demo of a not-yet-released song had been circulated on Napster. On the other hand, some lesser-known groups had welcomed the free distribution and publicity that Napster had provided for them, and had found that sales of their songs had increased. The downside to this was that the artists lost control of distribution. While several studies have been done on this issue, there had not been conclusive evidence to determine which side of this argument is correct.

Yet another angle of the argument is the ethical one. Some suggested that even though the songs were available free of charge on Napster, the consumer had an ethical obligation to purchase them.

The Recording Industry Association of America (RIAA) filed a lawsuit almost immediately after Napster went into business, with the goal of shutting Napster down because they claimed Napster was distributing copyrighted information. Napster's defense was that in the peer-to-peer system technically the consumers were the ones sharing the information with each other so it wasn't illegal. However, a court order in March 2001 restricted Napster from trading copyrighted material on its network and in order to comply with that order Napster shut down completely.

Napster then settled the case by paying fees and advance royalties. To support these debts Napster tried to change from a free service to a pay-service but was unsuccessful. After a couple of unsuccessful buyout bids, a company by the name of Roxio bought the Napster name and logo at a bankruptcy auction and used it to brand a subscription music service that is still in existence today.

While the Napster company story is an interesting one, what is perhaps the most significant thing about Napster is how it brought the MP3 file sharing debate to the forefront of the music industry. While the legal and ethical debate continues, what is clear to everyone is that peer-to-peer music file sharing is here to stay.

The success of Napster also spawned the development of legal digital music distribution. In 2006, estimates suggested that almost 140 million songs were downloaded per quarter. The most successful to date has been iTunes that has approximately 70 percent of the online song market—it is also the fourth largest leading music retailer overall. The second largest vendor is eMusic with a 10 percent share. Notably, other digital music distributors' products are not compatible with the iPod—the leading MP3 player.

The success of iTunes continues to attract other players to the market including Microsoft with Zune—a product that, like Apple, offers both hardware and software. Others such as Yahoo, Inc. are attempting to integrate their music products with other players such as cell phones. Those already in the market such as eMusic are offering customers that still buy CDs, CD-style packaging for some of their digital albums.

For many of the legal download music services the challenge continues to be how to acquire a large music database of material, how to extract payment for downloads, and then how to maintain and grow the customer base. Yahoo Music Unlimited's approach is to offer a subscription model that allows customers unlimited downloads for a flat monthly fee—but when the subscription ends the music literally stops playing. Microsoft's Zune offers individual songs for 99 cents, or an unlimited download subscription for about $15 a month.

See also: Innovation; Internet

Further Reading

"The Day the Napster Died," by Brad King, published in *Wired*, May 15, 2002 located on www.howstuffworks.com.
"How the Old Napster Worked," by Jeff Tyson, located online at www.how stuffworks.com.
www.napster.com

NASDAQ

The NASDAQ is one of the leading stock exchanges in the United States. The two primary stock markets are the NASDAQ (which accounts for more than 56 percent of total share volume traded) and the New York Stock Exchange, the NYSE or the Big Board (which accounts for about 37 percent of total share volume and has about 2,800 listed companies).

Traditionally, the NYSE has been viewed as the premier, venerable market that defined U.S. commerce, with the NASDAQ as a more brash upstart market. As such, many traditionally think of the NYSE as populated by the Blue Chip companies and the NASDAQ by technology companies. While this may be true, the NASDAQ has emerged as a substantive trading force that is home to over 3,200 companies.

The origins of the NASDAQ began in 1961 when the U.S. Congress authorized the Securities and Exchange Commission (SEC) to study fragmentation in the over the counter trading market. That study charged the National Association of Securities Dealers (NASD) to implement an automated solution. Ten years later the National Association of Securities Dealers Automated Quotations (NASDAQ) began trading; providing quotes for 2,500 over the counter securities. With continued investment in technology and outreach to companies anxious to trade publicly to raise capital, the NASDAQ continued to grow and innovate. In 1993 the market developed three new indexes to track growth industries: biotechnology, computers, and telecommunications. In 1994, the NASDAQ surpassed the NYSE in yearly stock volume, and in 1999 the NASDAQ became the world's biggest stock market by volume. In 2000 the NASDAQ membership voted to restructure the governance of the exchanges and spun off the NASDAQ into a shareholder-owned for-profit company. The NASDAQ is significantly different from the NYSE in several ways. For example, investors can trade stocks on any exchange, regardless of where the stock is listed. IBM stock is listed on the NYSE but could be traded on the NASDAQ or any other exchange. While the NASDAQ welcomes other stocks not listed with it, the NYSE trades few stocks that do not officially list on their own exchange.

The two exchanges also trade in different ways. On the NYSE, orders go to a "specialist" for each stock. The specialist works on the trading floor in New York, working to maintain a "fair and orderly market" for the stock. The specialist acts as the market maker (posting buy and selling quotes) and auctioneer (matching orders of customers sent to the NYSE floor). In general large orders are negotiated face-to-face while smaller orders are routed electronically to the specialist's order book. Access to the floor is limited to members who have a seat on the exchange. There are about 1,366 members and the cost of a seat is about $1.5 million.

By contrast, the NASDAQ's electronic market, given its origins is a "fully computerized" market with an open architecture. It has no specialists. Instead, NASDAQ operates a system, which includes approximately 300 market makers who compete in NASDAQ stocks. Orders are not in one central position; but are spread over many market makers, with over fifteen market makers in a given NASDAQ security. The market markers post their bid and ask prices into the NASDAQ network where they can be viewed by all participants. On average, there are sixty-seven market makers for NASDAQ-listed S&P 500 stocks. In the most active NASDAQ stocks, no market maker handles more than 3–5 percent of business in one stock at any time.

Traditionally the NASDAQ has been home to emerging companies and industries. For example, the NASDAQ 100 is approximately 57 percent technology companies, 20 percent consumer services, and 15 percent health care. Given its heavy technology weighting the NASDAQ was affected significantly by the Internet boom and subsequent bursting of the Internet bubble. In March 2000 the NASDAQ reached the peak of its upward momentum—an all time high of 5,132 an 88 percent increase from 1999. From that high in March, the index fell led by losses in technology, media, telecommunications, and Internet shares. As reported in the *New York Times* (December 30, 2000), the NASDAQ had its worst year since its founding with leading companies such as Dell Computer falling 66 percent and Microsoft 63 percent. Others fared even more poorly with Priceline.com falling 97 percent, Yahoo 86 percent, and Amazon.com 77 percent for the year.

Despite the hits taken by the NASDAQ in 2000, the market has rebounded. In 2004, the NASDAQ added 148 initial public offerings (IPOs), twenty-five of the new listing were foreign companies. It also traded 98.5 million shares daily on average, and had an average daily volume of $34.8 billion and an 8.8 trillion total dollar volume.

See also: Sarbanes–Oxley Act of 2002

Further Reading

www.nasdaq.com

National Secretaries Day

In 1952 Mary Barrett, president of The National Secretaries Association, a group of office product manufacturers, and Harry Klemfuss, public relations account executive at Young & Rubicam organized a "National Secretaries Week" campaign. The goal of the campaign was to recognize the work that secretaries did for organizations and promote how valuable they were to the organization. There was a shortage of skilled office labor at the time and this campaign was an effort to keep current secretaries in their jobs and encourage others to aspire to a secretarial career. National Secretaries Day was one specific day in the week on which to focus on the secretary.

The first National Secretary's Week was proclaimed by U.S. Secretary of Commerce Charles Sawyer as June 1–7, 1952, with the first National Secretaries Day being June 4, the Wednesday of that week. Two years later the National Secretaries Association changed the date of National Secretaries Week to be the last full week in April with National Secretaries Day falling on the Wednesday of that week, and that designation remains today.

While the dates and recognition remain constant, many things have changed about National Secretaries Day over the years as the role of the traditional secretary has evolved. The name was changed to Professional Secretaries Day in 1981 when the organization's name was changed to Professional Secretaries International (PSI). The organization's name was again changed in 1998 to the International Association of Administrative Professionals (IAAP) and in 2000 Professional Secretaries Day was changed to Administrative Professionals Day, the name that remains in effect today.

Popular myth holds that Administrative Professionals Day was created by greeting card companies, candy manufacturers, and florists for their own financial gain, and it is often referred to as a "Hallmark Holiday." In fact it was actually created by the organization charged with promoting Administrative Professionals and their careers. That being said, Administrative Professionals are often given gifts of cards, candy, and flowers during Administrative Professionals Week, or on Administrative Professionals Day so it is easy to see from where the myth originated.

While administrative professionals are often treated to lunch by their bosses on Administrative Professionals Day, the IAAP suggests that supervisors recognize Administrative Professionals " . . . by providing training for their administrative staff through seminars, continuing education, or self-study materials. Another suggestion is to make a commitment toward delegating responsibilities that better utilize the skills of administrative professionals."

See also: Performance Management/Performance Measurement

Further Reading

www.iaap-hq.org (International Association of Administrative Professionals)

Networking

In today's business culture networking is widespread. There is career networking, business networking, computer networking, network effects, peer to peer networks, dial-up networking, etc. What each of these terms have in common is the linking of different groups—people, groups, companies, or institutions—for the exchange of services, products, or information.

Clearly the best known opportunity for networking in recent years has been the Internet, providing the means for its 700 million users to connect, browse, and communicate. Information is exchanged, contacts are made, music is listened to, and business is transacted. The Center for Information and Research on Civic Learning and Engagement noted in 2004, that "The Internet has become a powerful force in political campaigns." Using the networking afforded by the Internet, young people had become engaged in the political process in "blogs, chat rooms, and meetings organized via the Internet." The most prominent use of Internet networking in politics was seen in former Vermont Governor Howard Dean's run for the Democratic presidential candidacy in 2003. Using the meetup .com website Dean was able to bring together over 30,000 supporters to his cause.

"It's not what you know, it's who you know," is the phrase most commonly associated with networking, applying not only to networking for a new job or career advancement but also to building sales. The reality is that all things being equal, people will hire or do business with people they know, like, and/or trust and networking is a means of building those relationships. To some extent, "the old boys network" and the "golf club

---

Why I Do This: Real Estate Brokers
Ed and Agnes Chatelain

We both have Master's degrees in archaeology/anthropology—it should be noted that our degrees predate the *Raiders of the Lost Arc* movies. Immediately after graduate school we both pursued careers in our chosen discipline—we both taught college courses and Ed worked as a county historical archaeologist and Agnes worked for the American Anthropological Society as a lobbyist.

After several years of working in our chosen careers we made a decision to pursue an entrepreneurial lifestyle. To this end we bought an ice cream shop and bakery in a resort community. We found that we enjoyed living in a small community and the additional freedom that being in one's own business provides.

While we had the ice cream store we constantly tinkered with the menus, rhw management styles, and explored a variety of aspects of the food service industry. Eventually, we felt that we had brought the business along as far as we were interested so we began searching for a new opportunity and settled on real estate sales.

The real estate industry encompasses a huge number of entrepreneurial opportunities, i.e., sales, rentals, new construction, renovation, commercial, industrial, and residential development to name a few. Also, the real estate industry affords one the opportunity to utilize all high school or college degrees, certifications, life experience, hobbies, interests, and intuitive knowledge that a person has developed. For instance, on any given day a real estate professional can be required to review plot plans, research deeds, discuss sales potential with architects and builders, price houses for homeowners, advise clients on interior design and landscaping, photograph houses, write advertising copy, and a myriad of other things. Real estate is a dynamic fast changing business in which any person can find a niche if they are interested in working hard. Finally, the real estate industry directly rewards competence, diligence, and hard work by providing direct compensation and the opportunity to make one's own hours and pursue one's own lifestyle as long as one is self motivated. As a result, we have happily pursued our careers in real estate and continue to find it interesting, satisfying, and lucrative.

---

network" still exist, so many believe that networking is especially important for those outside those networks to build relationships and trust.

When looking for a new job or advancing in an existing career, networking might entail making a list of the people that you know personally or professionally, meeting with them, and seeking their counsel about those opportunities or industries that might be the best fit for you and your aspirations. For college graduates, the alumni network is often an additional source of material. Often graduates of a school will offer to provide guidance and information, though not a job offer. For others, belonging to a professional organization can provide access to individuals that might be helpful in creating a network to mentor and direct an individual in their next career move.

In sales, one of the best prospects is a referral from someone within their network. If a sales rep has a large and diverse group of referrals, he or she is more likely to meet their sales goals. For example, in financial services once an advisor has established a relationship with a client, they might well ask if that person knows others that might be interested in financial advice. If the advisor receives such a referral he is more likely to be able to sell the business, because that person has a relationship with the originating customer and assumes a level of trust and competency in the reps offerings.

There are numerous books and articles on the art of networking—and that is a gross understatement. To quote just one, consider Stacey L. Bradford's article, entitled "Experts Offer Their Tips for Fruitful Networking" (published in the *Wall Street Journal* Online, at www.careerjournal.com), "When it comes to finding a job, nothing beats good, old-fashioned networking—contacting friends, relatives, and former colleagues, setting up face-to-face meetings in the hope of getting job referrals. Yes, it is awkward, but here's why it simply has to be done: At any given time, about 80 percent of all available jobs aren't posted in the classifieds or on job boards, says BH Careers International, a New York career-management firm. And 60 percent of people surveyed by BH said they got their last job by networking." There's incentive.

See also: Headhunter; War for Talent

Further Reading

Dig Your Well Before You're Thirsty: The Only Networking Book You'll Ever Need, by Harvey Mackay, Currency, 1st Currency pbk. ed. (February 16, 1999).

Signs of Changing Culture:
At Work, "Nice" is on the Rise. In a Huge Shift from the "Me First," "Greed is Good" Attitudes of the 1980s, Corporations Seek a Kinder, Gentler Culture

By Marilyn Gardner, Staff writer of *The Christian Science Monitor*. Reproduced with permission from the October 16, 2006 issue of *The Christian Science Monitor* (www.csmonitor.com). © 2006 *The Christian Science Monitor*. All rights reserved.

Patrick Morris could call it "a tale of two companies." As a new college graduate beginning his first job in public relations at a major cosmetics firm in New York, he knew he would be the proverbial low man on the totem pole.

"You feel you're going to get put upon and crunched and tossed around," he says. But instead of the huge egos and "attitude" he expected, he found himself surrounded by good, caring people. "It made all the difference in the world and helped to shape me into the professional I am today."

By contrast, his next job at a television shopping channel proved to be "an environment full of finger-pointing and backstabbing," he says. "It became a nightmare to go into the office."

In comic strips and movies, tyrannical bosses produce plenty of laughs. Think of Mr. Dithers, Dagwood Bumstead's nemesis in *Blondie*, or Miranda in *The Devil Wears Prada*. But in real life, managers like these are hardly funny.

Today, in a competitive age that sometimes takes a "nice guys finish last" approach to business, a quiet cultural change appears to be under way. "Nice" and "kind" are becoming operative philosophies in some companies, among them Mr. Morris's first employer. Those adjectives are also showing up in titles of books and organizations. They stand in sharp contrast to the 1980s, when a "greed is good" attitude prevailed in some quarters and business books carried titles such as "Corporate Combat" and "Office Warfare."

"There's a huge shift we've observed," says Russ Edelman, one of the founders of Nice Guy Strategies, a consulting firm in Newburyport, Mass. "Companies are fundamentally saying, 'We need to employ more ethical practices as well as create an environment that supports a nicer

mind-set.' Organizations are asking, 'How can we create an environment that is friendly, welcoming, and warm, but also ensure that people
in the company are held accountable and can achieve success?' There's
a balance people are struggling with."

Workplace observers attribute some of the changes to a reaction
against corporate scandals at Enron and Tyco. "In the past decade there
have been a lot of egomaniacal bosses," says Tim Hiltabiddle, one of
Mr. Edelman's business partners. Sept. 11 also heightened the yearning
for a kinder workplace, he says.

Yet that approach is "not about everything being nicey-nice," Mr. Hiltabiddle emphasizes. Nor does it mean being wimpy and naive, lacking
backbone, or serving as a doormat. Being too nice, in fact, carries its own
perils. "People might take advantage of your good nature," he says.

As one way of framing the issue, Hiltabiddle and Edelman sat down in
a restaurant and drew up a Nice Guys Bill of Rights on napkins. Those
rights include speaking up, setting boundaries, taking risks, valuing your
time, and being accountable. Studies show that niceness can also produce
bottom-line rewards, such as increasing productivity and reducing turnover, says Robin Koval, an advertising executive in New York and coauthor, with Linda Kaplan Thaler, of *The Power of Nice: How to Conquer
the Business World With Kindness* (Doubleday). Being nice, she adds, can
mean "having the courage and creativity to stand up for what you want,
but doing it in a way that is not ugly or threatening."

Women, Ms. Koval finds, are typically taught the importance of being
nice. That can produce stereotypes. Noting the popularity of the book,
Nice Girls Don't Get the Corner Office, she says, "We take issue with
that. We think we're nice girls, and we have corner offices."

For men, nice is a more liberating idea, Koval adds. "They're the ones
who have been socialized to think, 'I've got to be a tough guy, never
show my emotions, it's a dog-eat-dog world out there.'"

But "dog eat dog" isn't the only modus operandi. "To be successful
in business, you need to have a certain threshold of knowledge of your
industry and techniques," says Peter Handal, CEO of Dale Carnegie
Training in New York. "But it's not enough just to be good at what you
do. In my experience, the people who reach the top are nice. They're
people-friendly. They're ones who can communicate with people
around them, up and down."

They're also the ones who avoid what Duane Boyce, author of *The

Anatomy of Peace, calls "false niceness." He explains the term this way: "If I'm not focused on results, I'm just expecting my friendliness, my politeness to get me by. That's not nice."

In the political arena, this is shaping up to be another season filled with harsh campaign ads as candidates trade jibes and paint negative images of their opponents.

"It's so disheartening that election after election becomes about tearing down the other person," Hiltabiddle says. "It's not constructive in building something; it's tearing down."

Yet politics creates unique challenges. Assuming the role of a politician, Mr. Handal says, "The way I get ahead is either I sell people on me, or I knock you. There's only a binary choice. In business or nonprofits, there are lots of choices.

"Who moves up in organizations? People who are liked."

Customer service is another field filled with negative images. "People are tired of the indifference that we're receiving from so many companies these days in the name of customer service," says Ed Horrell, author of *The Kindness Revolution: The Company-wide Culture Shift That Inspires Phenomenal Customer Service*. He notes that consumers want service "peppered with some respect and dignity and kindness."

Mr. Horrell praises companies known for excellent service, such as Nordstrom, FedEx, L.L. Bean, and Chick-Fil-A. Their emphasis on core values—dignity, respect, courtesy, kindness—begins at the top and requires commitment from the CEO and managers all the way down to front-line workers. "The way they treat their employees is virtually always the way they'll treat their customers."

For Morris, the publicist who tells the tale of two very different companies, the positive examples set by his bosses and co-workers at the cosmetics firm continue to influence his work as public relations director of his firm in Troy, N.Y.

"If you want people to perform, and you want people to do a good job, you have to treat them nicely," he says. "It's not to say you don't lose your cool sometimes. But if somebody makes a mistake, what's not going to help them is to have an intensely negative reaction to it. What's going to help is to say, 'How do you think this happened? What do you think we should do to fix it? What steps should we take next time that this doesn't become a problem?' That's the way I was taught."

That kind of approach can pay big dividends. Pamela Gregg of the University of Dayton Research Institute in Ohio praises her bosses for "going out of their way to be nice to those around them." In addition to being fair and expressing appreciation for jobs well done, she says, they give employees "free rein to take risks and make what we can of our jobs."

Everyone works hard, Ms. Gregg says, so her bosses often lighten the mood with levity. One employee will soon celebrate forty-five years with the institute. For others, twenty, thirty, and forty years of service are not uncommon. Last year the *Dayton Business Journal* rated it one of the Top 10 winners in its "Best Places to Work in the Miami Valley" contest.

In an era of corporate downsizing, even cutbacks offer an opportunity for companies to soften their approach. "The act of laying someone off does not mean you're unkind," Horrell says. "A kind person does not want to do that, but there's a kind way to do it."

Making a case that "nice is very powerful," Koval says, "We all have to network with each other. We all work in teams. Unless you're a chemist in a lab bent over a test tube, nobody works alone. The old command-and-control way of doing business is clearly over." She adds, "Meanness is so last millennium. Niceness is the future."

Offshoring

When a U.S. company either opens a unit outside of the borders of the United States to manufacture goods or to conduct services, or hires another company outside of the United States to do those things, it is called offshoring. Generally, companies "offshore" work to take advantage of lower-cost labor in other countries.

One of the pioneers of offshore outsourcing was Jack Welch. While CEO of General Electric in the early 1990s, Welch introduced a new rule for GE's offshore activities called the 70:70:70 rule. In a communication to employees, "Welch mandated that 70 percent of GE's work would be outsourced. Out of this, 70 percent of that work would be completed from offshore development centers. And out of this, about 70 percent would be sent to India. This comes out to about 30 percent of GE's work being outsourced to India" (EBS, www.ebstrategy.com/oursing/basics/definition.htm) The success of GE and other companies marked a continued interest in offshoring.

In recent years, as the quality of education and expertise has increased in developing countries like India and China, more U.S. companies have been offshoring (and outsourcing) work. Earlier waves of offshoring primarily encompassed manufacturing and blue collar works but, in recent years, offshoring has come to include, increasingly, service capabilities that require well-educated employees. For example, as noted in *Fortune* (July 25, 2005), "Texas Instruments is conducting critical parts of its next-generation chip development—extraordinarily complex work on which the company is betting its future—in India. American computer programmers who made $100,000 a year or more are getting fired because Indians and Chinese do the same work for one-fifth the cost or less."

The McKinsey Global Institute predicts that some industries could be profoundly changed: For example, "in packaged software worldwide, 49 percent of jobs could in theory be outsourced to low-wage countries; in infotech services, 44 percent. In other industries the potential job shifts are smaller but still so large they'd create major dislocations: Some 25 percent of worldwide banking jobs could be sent offshore, 19 percent of insurance jobs, 13 percent of pharmaceutical jobs. Further 52 percent of engineering jobs and 31 percent of accounting jobs could be offshored. (Source: "America Isn't Ready [Here's What To Do About It]," *Fortune*, July 25, 2005.)

That same McKinsey study calculated almost 10 million U.S. service jobs could be subject to offshoring—should that occur it would result in the U.S. unemployment rate climbing from 5 percent to 11.4 percent. But estimates suggest that only 40 percent of those jobs will ultimately be offshored from high-wage countries to low-wage countries by 2008. Forrester Research puts the number at 3.4 million white-collar jobs by 2015. Researchers at the University of California at Berkeley believe the number will be far larger, perhaps 14 million.

Yet, when a company makes a decision to offshore a business or a business process, it is not a guarantee to make a profit. As Ravi Avon and Jitendra V. Singh, note in the *Harvard Business Review* article, "Getting Offshoring Right," "It's not easy to make money by offshoring business processes, many CEO's are discovering. Companies benefit only when they pick the right processes, calculate both the operational and structural risks, and match organizational forms to meet needs." In other cases, companies can be profitable but choose to scale back offshoring when it meets with customer dissatisfaction. For example, in 2003, in response to complaints about customer service calls, Dell selectively chose to bring back some of its overseas business customer service in Texas, Idaho, and Tennessee from sites in India.

See also: Outsourcing

Further Reading

Offshoring: Understanding the Emerging Global Labor Market (McKinsey Global Institute), by Diana Farrell (ed.), Harvard Business School Press (December 19, 2006).

Ombudsman

An ombudsman is an official who investigates complaints made against a group or organization by people outside that group or organization. The ombudsman sometimes follows his/her investigation with mediation to obtain a resolution of the complaint. Ombudsmen exist in three main environments: government and corporate organizations, non-corporate organizations, and the news media.

While ombudsmen have been found in history dating back to the Qin Dynasty in China, their modern use stems from Sweden where they have been used successfully in the Swedish Parliament since the early 1800s. Many other countries have ombudsmen, but none have been as successful at implementing the role as the Scandinavians.

The term ombudsman is derived from the Norse word, *umbodhsmadhr,* a non-gender-specific term meaning deputy. It is therefore correct to use ombudsman as a gender-neutral word, but equally correct to refer to someone as an ombudswoman, or a group as ombudspeople if the situation warrants.

Most ombudsman offices have a stated procedure that is used to submit a complaint, and a prescribed course of action that the ombudsman follows once a complaint has been submitted. Regardless of the system, the ombudsman thoroughly investigates the issues and communicates with all those involved.

Ombudsmen are most frequently found in government where they represent the rights of the citizens with respect to governmental issues. While these ombudsmen are typically appointed by a government official, their main focus is to investigate complaints brought by citizens against the government or governmental agency.

An example of a governmental ombudsman is the Office of the National Ombudsman with the U.S. Small Business Administration, whose mission is " . . . to assist small businesses when they experience excessive federal regulatory enforcement actions, such as repetitive audits or investigations, excessive fines, penalties, threats, retaliation, or other unfair enforcement action by a federal agency."

Other ombudsman offices that assist the general public are those such as the Long Term Care Ombudsman and the Foster Care Ombudsman.

In both corporate and noncorporate organizations the ombudsman is charged with investigating complaints against the organization made by

Why I Do This: Director, Public Records and Open Public Meetings
Eliza Saunders

I work for the largest public research university in the United States. I am the chief compliance officer for the freedom of information and the open public meetings acts. What does this mean? We get requests from the public, asking for records, and we make sure that the university gives out what is legally releaseable.

So if someone asks, for example, to have copies of all emails from a particular Dean for a given time period, my staff gets them, and then reads them and "redacts" information—that is, takes information out—as allowed by the law. We do this for any kind of record—any information in any format. It could be a database, it could be performance evaluations, whatever.

How did I find this job? I was working in the IT department, and someone literally came up to me and asked me to consider this job.

My background includes working for the registrar's office at Boston University; I have also been the administrator of admissions at the Harvard Medical School; I've worked in the financial industry and in the health care field.

I have a master's degree in public relations, which oddly enough helps a lot in this field, because most of our more complicated requests come from the media or from attorneys. It helps to be familiar with working as an "external contact" for a company.

You might like this job if you're detail oriented, if you're good at identifying problems, and if you can handle working in high pressure situations with high level executives. You also have to be able to handle quiet. It's dead quiet in my office most of the time. And, you also have to love to read and do research.

employees within the organization. An organizational ombudsman mediates resolutions to the issues investigated more often than ombudsmen do in government.

An organizational ombudsman works for the organization, and is usually high-ranking but is not part of the management team. In order to more easily remain neutral, the ombudsman often reports directly to the Board of Directors and not to management. Examples of types of complaints that would be brought to an organizational ombudsman include (but are not limited to): Fair Employment Practices, Harassment, Environmental Health and Safety, Supplier Relationships, and Petty Theft. An ombudsman provides a means through which a whistleblower can voice their concerns.

The first North American news ombudsman was appointed at the *Courier-Journal* in Louisville, Kentucky in 1967. Sometimes referred to as "readers representatives," the job of the news ombudsman is to review customer's complaints and work to find a satisfactory resolution. These complaints can range from comments about news accuracy, to ethics, to fairness in reporting.

The recently appointed ombudsman (as of this writing) at National Public Radio (NPR) stated his task as follows: "My mission is to listen to your concerns, criticisms, and compliments about National Public Radio's shows and to communicate those issues to the NPR staff. My commitment to you is to take your concerns seriously, to attempt to get answers to your questions, responses to your comments, and to write a column based on those conversations and the reporting I do after we've talked."

The majority of today's U.S. news ombudsmen work for newspapers, with others representing the public's concerns at radio and television networks. It is important to note, however, that there are many fewer news organizations *without* an ombudsman than there are *with* an ombudsman.

There are a number of trade organizations for Ombudsmen such as the Organization of News Ombudsmen (ONO), The International Ombudsman Association (IOA), and the International Ombudsman Institute (IOI) to name a few. These organizations provide seminars, information, and a forum through which ombudsmen can discuss issues with each other, such as maintaining neutrality and ways to handle angry callers.

In business there have been formal or informal ombudsman roles, where employees can go to an impartial party to discuss problems and complaints. At times a formal role has been created following crisis in a business. For example, British Petroleum (BP) created a new ombudsman position in its U.S. division shortly after problems in Alaska at Prudhoe Bay. At BP the ombudsman staff operated a twenty-four hour telephone service that workers could call to report complaints. The BP ombudsman described his job in the *Wall Street Journal* (September 5, 2006) as to "do whatever is necessary to ascertain the facts about and identify the solutions for problems that exist today as well as those likely to become issues in the future."

Regardless of their environment, the major issue facing ombudsmen is how to remain neutral, and perhaps more importantly how to maintain the image of remaining neutral, as they investigate issues such as harassment, or other unethical charges that can often be very polarizing. Essentially, their job is to investigate and sometimes criticize their own employer. In order to maintain their neutrality, ombudsmen follow strict procedures and focus on being extremely thorough.

See also: Suggestion Box

Further Reading

Conflict Resolution and the Ombudsman: A Bibliography on the Ombudsman Concept in the Corporate, University and Medical Environments, by Laura Ferris Brown, Library and Information Center on the Resolution of Disputes, American Arbitration Association (1993).

One-to-One Marketing

When a company is communicating with a single customer at a time, and tailoring their interaction to suit that particular customer's needs, it is called one-to-one marketing.

Put another way, in the field of marketing, one-to-one marketing means developing a relationship with a customer and tailoring products and services to that customer—customization for a customer of one. The idea is that when the company engages the customer in a meaningful dialogue, they will develop products and services more meaningful to that customer and gain a greater and greater share of that customer's total purchases.

Many companies have discovered that actually executing such a marketing plan is challenging. As some of the best known champions of one-to-one marketing, Don Peppers and Martha Rogers, noted in the article, "Is Your Company Ready for One-to-One Marketing? (*Harvard Business Review*, January–February 1999), "The mechanics of implementation are complex. It's one thing to train a sales staff to be warm and attentive, it's quite another to identify, track, and interact with an individual customer and then reconfigure your product or service to meet that customer's needs."

The authors advocate four steps in the creation of a successful one-to-one marketing program: "identifying customers, differentiating among them, interacting with them, and customize your product or service to meet each customer's needs." A company's readiness for a one-to-one marketing program is then dependent on the company's ability to know its customers, be able to differentiate their needs, interact with them, and customize products or services for them. While this seems relatively simple, there are potential roadblocks. For example, some companies do not sell their products directly to customers (the end-user) but rather sell through a retail network. As a result they may not know their customers nor be in a position to interact with them.

Technology has been a facilitator of many one-to-one marketing programs. E-mail allows companies to contact customers directly and sell to them based on their recorded purchase histories. Advanced software programs like Customer Relationship Management (CRM) track customer history and purchase patterns. Companies, like Dell, use technology to allow customers to customize their computers in the purchase process. Amazon.com, the online store, uses past purchase history to offer customers complementary products when the customer first logs onto its site.

Despite its benefits, one-to-one marketing has its drawbacks. As Paul Nunes and Jeffrey Merrihue noted in "The Continuing Power of Mass Advertising" (*MIT Sloan Management Review*, Winter 2007), "While the 'market of one' approach can pay off, it requires significant upfront investment including: implementing customer relationship management software applications; filtering, enhancing and cleaning customer data; and personalizing interactions (e-mail, billing, offers, and so on). These activities take time and coordination of multiple parts of the organization (marketing, customer service, sales, information technology), which for companies that are trying to be highly reactive to changing environment, can be daunting."

Overall critics suggest that one-to-one marketing is expensive and needs to be better integrated into an overall marketing strategy that selectively combines one-to-one marketing with one-to-many marketing tactics.

See also: The 4Ps; Relationship Marketing

Further Reading

The One to One Future, by Don Peppers and Martha Rogers, Currency, 1st Currency pbk. ed. (December 14, 1996).

Open Book Management

The management concept of Open Book Management implies that a company's financials are available for any employee to see. It also implies that employees are going to need to understand what they see; it's up to them to make those numbers improve.

Open Book Management might be compared to a student whose teacher announced an "open-book" test. It is likely that the student would feel relief at not having to memorize everything quickly. And that relief may then morph into the realization that the student would now have to know how to find all of the answers quickly and effectively so they could finish the test on time and with the correct answers.

To a certain extent, this mingled relief and pressure are felt by employees often when they learn they are going to work for a company that practices Open Book Management, or that their current company is going to change to Open Book Management. Elation comes at the idea that they are going to have access to all of the financial documents of the company followed by either the fear that it is "just talk and no substance" or the realization that they are going to have to *understand* those financials.

Open Book Management as a term was used by John Case, who was a senior writer at *Inc.* magazine in 1995 when he coined the phrase, according to www.inc.com. Case went on to write a book on the topic, entitled *Open-Book Management: The Coming Business Revolution* (Collins paperback reprint, May 1996). In it, he described the approach, and also discussed the work of Jack Stack. Stack pioneered the approach—though it wasn't called Open Book Management at the time—when he became the new plant manager at SRC, a failing division of International Harvester. Stack had an idea that if each and every employee at SRC had access to the numbers, a vested interest in the numbers, and the power to affect the numbers, then those employees would work harder to ensure that those "numbers" improved, and that profitability would increase. With that approach as a lynchpin of his strategy, Stack and twelve other employees purchased the business from International Harvester in 1983.

Getting disconcerted line employees who were considering voting in a union to believe that they could contribute more to the company and thus manage their own futures was no easy task. However, by training employees on how to read financial statements, determining goals for each area of the company, and then rewarding employees when those goals were met, Stack *did* turn SRC around. Stack viewed business as a "game" and one that he wanted to win. He presented the "Great Game of Business" (his term) to the workers at SRC by determining a number that each area needed to achieve in order to win the game. These numbers were derived from what the company actually needed to achieve to improve its profitability. Then, in order to ensure that everyone understood the "game," he provided training courses for everyone to attend that would teach them to understand the numbers.

Because he worked in manufacturing, the "numbers" were not always sales related. For example, sometimes the number was for safety—like reducing the number of accidents, or the number might be related to equipment needs—like determining whether to repair or replace a piece of equipment. Rewards for meeting the goal started small and got larger as the goals became larger. Eventually, he even had employees involved in rewriting the compensation plan.

One of the keys to his success was also his willingness to communicate with employees. Not only did he talk with them one-on-one, and listen when they talked, he also implemented stock-ticker-like boards in each area of the company—even the cafeteria—so that the employees would be able to see at all times how they were doing compared to their goal. He and the other managers and supervisors at SRC even made it a habit to hang out at a local pool bar every afternoon from 4–6 P.M. where employees could talk with them in a more casual setting—over a game of pool.

The success of Open Book Management at SRC was not just from showing employees the company's statistics. It was a complete change in the culture of the company from one where the workers just worked to receive their paycheck, to one where the workers worked for themselves—their compensation plan included an Employee Stock Ownership Plan (ESOP). Presented with the opportunity and the power to affect the company's revenues, workers believed in Jack and his plan, which lead to success for everyone.

Implementing Open Book Management is not something that can be done easily, nor is it something that can be accomplished overnight. It takes a great deal of commitment by management to effect the culture change necessary in order for it to work. Many companies that consider changing to Open Book Management are doing so as a "last resort." They are failing and have tried every other management tool that they know of without success, so they turn to this as their last gasp, so to speak. This means that employees are usually disgruntled, sometimes overworked, and don't necessarily trust the management team to begin with. These are large hurdles over which the management team needs to jump before they can begin to see an improvement.

However, the commitment to success can pay off. After a company gives employees the training they need in order to understand their goals, and the power to make changes in their work for the success of the company, it is up to each and every employee to "buy in" to the concept and apply themselves to learning and improving. Provided they do this, everyone wins in the Great Game of Business.

As John Case put it, "The beauty of open-book management is that it really works. It helps companies compete in today's mercurial marketplace by getting everybody on the payroll thinking and acting like a businessperson, an owner, rather than like a traditional hired hand" (www.inc.com/guides/leadership_strat).

See also: Learning Organization

Further Reading

"Communication: Open-Book Management 101: The Story of How One Company Embraced Open-Book Management and What Affect It Had on the Staff," by Donna Fenn in Inc.com, published August 1996, on www.inc.com.

Outsourcing

Outsourcing, sometimes called "contracting out," is a relatively new function of modern-day business and started in the 1980s. Outsourcing refers to the practice of transferring the supplier of some products or services from inside the organization to outside the organization. Key to the definition of outsourcing is that the *control* of the function being outsourced is also given to the outside organization.

A report of the Panel of the National Academy of Public Administration in January 2006 defines outsourcing as follows: "Outsourcing refers to a business restructuring or change in current business practice that shifts operations or processes previously performed within the company to an outside entity—an independent third party." Outsourcing can be established with a company in the original company's country or outside that country. When performed with a company outside the country it is often referred to as "Offshore Outsourcing."

The move toward flexible work schedules and the concept of "working from home" that has developed in the past decade or so has supplied the workforce with many well-qualified professionals who can perform contract services to a variety of companies. Technology advances have made this source of outsourcing possible in a way that never existed before.

Some of the benefits of outsourcing include lower labor cost, better product quality, more efficiency, and increased productivity. Critics of outsourcing cite concern with whether or not product quality is really improved, the decrease in jobs for local laborers—both blue and white collar, and customer security issues. Indeed, there was a well-publicized case in 2005 where several employees in India outsourced by Citibank were able to hack into the Citibank database and steal $350,000 from customer accounts.

It seems that both sides of the outsourcing debate have validity. While there are certainly companies that have benefited both financially and organizationally, a number of companies also report that their results from outsourcing were not as phenomenal as they had expected due to poor quality or other manufacturing or communication issues.

Many companies outsource in more than one area. For example, a company that manufactures art supplies and sells them at wholesale to retail stores might find that it has lower production costs if it outsources the manufacture of its items to China. China's per piece cost to manufacture the art supplies is so much less than the cost to manufacture the same supplies in the United States, that even when you take shipping costs into account, it costs less to have them manufactured in China than the United States. That very same company may find that it is also more expensive to have local labor receive, pack, and ship their products from their corporate headquarters than it would be to have the products shipped to a fulfillment company in the United States and have the orders sent to the retail stores directly from there, leaving only the design, administrative, and corporate divisions in residence at the company's headquarters.

With outsourcing, the traditional roles of business entities are changed significantly. An expanded level of trust must be established between the companies doing business with each other in this fashion. Consider the example above in which the art supply company is actually giving the fulfillment company confidential information about their customers, orders, and delivery that were unheard of before the advent of outsourcing.

For the first twenty years or so that companies were outsourcing, the jobs that were outsourced were mainly blue collar and low paid positions. While this caused concern among some labor groups that local jobs were being lost, companies were able to continue outsourcing because the lower costs simply made them more competitive, allowing them to charge less or make greater profits on their sales.

Today more white collar research and development (R&D) and technical jobs are being outsourced, which is causing a much larger uproar in the business community as companies are divided about the advisability of this. One of the most visible examples of outsourcing R&D is how many of the large technology companies are purchasing completed designs for digital products (like cell phones and MP3 players) from Asian companies, changing them only slightly to meet the U.S. consumer's needs (and in some cases not changing them at all) and then putting their own brand name on them. U.S. consumers rarely know who designed the products they are purchasing. This type of outsourcing is not limited to technology however. Pharmaceutical companies, airline manufacturers, and biotech companies are taking advantage of lower R&D costs for outsourced design as well.

China and India both have a large number of engineers who work for lower wages than their U.S. counterparts, and are hotbeds of what is being termed "intellectual property" that they can market to large corporations. Advances in technology over the past several years have fueled their marketability because it is now possible to work and communicate over the internet and e-mail without having to physically be in the same location. It is for these reasons that many companies outsource to China and India.

Some say that Research & Design (R&D) will become the "next manufacturing" and that in the not-too-distant future, companies will be restructuring again and this time instead of outsourcing just manufacturing, they will be outsourcing R&D as well. Others, like Apple Computer, contend that outsourcing all of a company's R&D will lead to a competitive disadvantage and they insist upon keeping R&D in-house.

Regardless of the extent to which a company outsources, the concept is here to stay and when managed well, can prove to be a financial win for both companies involved.

See also: Core Competencies

Further Reading

"The Future of Outsourcing," by Pete Engardio, with Michael Arndt in Green Bay, Wis., and Dean Foust in Charlotte, N.C., a special report in *Business Week*, January 30, 2006, located on www.businessweek.com.

Performance Management/ Performance Measurement

There is a saying in business, "that if something is not measured it does not get done," hence the need for performance measurement and performance management. Generally speaking, there are two types of performance measurement: measurement of the performance of the organization and measurement of the people within it. While both have qualitative and quantitative aspects to them, the measurement of the organization's performance tends to be more quantitative and objective, while measuring the performance of people is more qualitative and subjective.

One of the most important measures of an organization's performance is how it is doing financially. A company's financial statements are the best known measures of its financial performance. There are three major financial statements. The first of these is the balance sheet, which provides a "snapshot" of the company at a point in time—usually its year end. The balance sheet lists the organization's assets, liabilities, and the level of shareholder equity in the enterprise. The second financial indicator is the income statement, which summarizes performance over a period of time. It begins with the revenues earned in the period and subtracts the costs to determine the income of the business. Finally, the statement of financial position provides insight into how cash flowed in and out of the business during the year.

For publicly-traded companies, the performance indicated by their financial statements has an almost immediate impact on their value. Earnings are announced quarterly, and if the company "beats" market expectations the price of its stock tends to rise. Conversely, when a company fails to meet earnings expectation, the stock price falls. As stock performance is tied to executive compensation, senior executives in organizations spend significant time trying to align market expectation and company performance. Some industry observers suggest that too much time is focused on meeting quarterly performance expectations at the price of long-term strategy—indeed, that managers are working to "meet the numbers" rather than increase the value of the business.

The data in the financial statements provide the basis for a vast amount of performance analysis, including financial ratios such as return on assets, return on investment, and gross margins, that are used to determine the viability and strength of the organization. For the markets to operate efficiently, there has to be trust in the reporting system. The Securities and Exchange Commission (SEC) has authority for establishing accounting and reporting standards under the Securities and Exchange Act of 1934. The SEC has recognized the standards of the Financial Accounting Standards Board (FASB) in the preparation of financial statements, and companies adhere to those rules in the preparation of financial statements. While most would agree that the performance presented in financial statements is reliable, there have been notable scandals involving Enron, dating of stock options of executives, etc.

In addition to financial statements that report performance to an external audience, there are a host of internal performance measures. Some companies, for example, will use a "balanced scorecard" approach to internal performance management. Developed by Robert Kaplan and David Norton, this approach attempts to balance a company's financial measurements—which "tell the story of past events," according to Kaplan and Norton—with three additional perspectives: the Learning and Growth Perspective, the Business Process Perspective, and the Customer Perspective. The Learning and Growth Perspective has to do generally with a company's ability to change and adapt over time; the Business Process Perspective is all about those processes at which the company expects to excel; and the Customer Perspective is about a company's appearance to customers. Through measuring all four dimensions, a company can hope to improve itself on many levels, not just the financial.

Another level of performance measurement and management is at the individual level. In order to fairly compensate employees and set expectations for them, companies provide ongoing employee appraisals. Many establish a performance plan for employees that is aligned with the goals and objectives of the organization. The performance plan calls for the development of certain competencies and achievement of defined objectives.

GE is generally perceived to be a leader in performance management. Under the direction of then CEO Jack Welch, GE began an aggressive performance review system that identified and gave bonuses to the top 20 percent of employees; over time those identified as the bottom 20 percent left the company—voluntarily or involuntarily. The result was a culture that was performance driven with "dead weight" constantly removed and the talent pool constantly improved.

Most companies will conduct an annual formal performance review of employee's achievements against their performance plan. Traditionally, it entails self-evaluation by the employee and a separate evaluation by the supervisor. The two individuals then meet and review performance. Both parties sign the review to indicate agreement on the performance and often use the session to set goals for the next fiscal year. Often too the performance on the appraisal is used to determine the variable (bonus) part of compensation. More recently, companies have begun using a 360-degree appraisal process in which an evaluation form is sent to peers and subordinates beyond the individual and the supervisor.

Ultimately, both performance measurement and management are important for a company's continued health and success—much as seeing a doctor for a regular check-up is important for us as individuals. While the system can be abused, e.g., with managers focusing on immediate fixes and not long-term success, performance tools provide an overall map on which to chart progress, and even help determine steps to be taken in the here and now to help the body corporate carry on to a healthy and profitable future.

See also: Benchmarking; General Electric (GE) Workout; Management by Objectives; 360-Degree Feedback

Further Reading

www.worldatwork.org

Signs of Changing Culture:
Most Companies Are Only Moderately Successful—Or Worse—
When It Comes to Executing Strategy, Executives Say

New York, March 19, 2007

Few executives (3 percent) say their companies are very successful at executing corporate strategies, while the majority (62 percent) admit that their organizations are only moderately successful—or worse—at strategy execution. That's according to a new global survey commissioned by American Management Association (AMA) and conducted by the Human Resource Institute (HRI).

The AMA/HRI survey "The Keys to Strategy Execution" included responses from 1,526 managers and HR experts from around the world. The survey was conducted in conjunction with AMA's affiliates and global partners, including Canadian Management Centre in Toronto, Management Centre Europe in Brussels, AMA Latin America in Mexico City, and AMA Asia in Tokyo.

"Our survey found that executives and managers are trained to plan strategies, but believe they often fall short in execution due to a lack of skills and the existence of a process to facilitate implementation of plans," said Edward T. Reilly, AMA's president and CEO. "The findings show that strategy execution can improve as executives learn how to focus and align daily activities to strategic goals. To ensure this, top leaders must be committed to clear, direct, and constant communication, and committed to the change necessary to implement evolving strategies," Reilly said.

The companies that reported relatively high success at executing strategies, however, seem to reap real dividends. That is, organizations that were good at executing strategies were also more likely to cite success in the marketplace, as measured by self-reported revenue growth, market share, profitability, and customer satisfaction.

The AMA/HRI survey gauged respondents' ability to implement strategies in two ways: by asking them to rate their execution success and by asking them about the extent to which they use and value fifty-seven different strategy-implementation practices. The research found that, above all else, clarity of communication is crucial to the execution of strategy.

The pivotal role of clarity was demonstrated by the fact that "creating a clear strategy" was ranked as the single most important practice. What's more, out of fifty-seven different approaches to strategy execution, "defining clear goals to support strategy," "ensuring clear accountability" and "having a clear focus on implementing/executing strategy" were among the top six important practices.

The problem, however, is that organizations are not achieving clarity to the degree they should. Although clear strategies and clear goals were of top importance, they were only ranked eleventh and tenth in terms of the extent to which companies use those approaches. There was a particularly large difference between the extent to which companies value a clear strategy and the extent to which they actually deliver a clear strategy.

As might be expected, companies that perform better in the marketplace are much more likely than lower performers to provide clarity. In fact, out of the top six major areas of difference between higher and lower performers, three of them (clear strategy, clear goals, and clear focus) deal with clarity.

Another major finding of the survey is that alignment practices are widely used and highly valued among responding organizations. Alignment practices account for four out of the top ten most commonly used strategy execution methods. They are also among the top ten most highly valued practices. Among the most highly ranked practices are "aligning strategy with the corporate vision/mission statement," "aligning organizational goals with strategy," "aligning business units' goals with organizational goals," and "aligning business units with strategy."

Higher-performing organizations are considerably more likely than other organizations to use certain alignment strategies. Specifically, higher performers are more likely to align organizational goals with strategy and to align incentives, rewards, and recognition with strategy.

Speed and adaptability are also differentiators between higher and lower market performers. To a much greater extent than lower performers, higher performers demonstrate "the ability to quickly and effectively execute when new strategic opportunities arise." Another differentiator is "having an adaptive organizational infrastructure." These findings suggest that adaptive organizational infrastructures—in combination with clarity and alignment—help organizations react more quickly to new strategic opportunities.

Leadership practices also influence strategy execution, but there seems to be an overall leadership development deficit in this area. Organizations do not build "execution-focused leadership capabilities" or use "succession planning to develop leaders who are good at strategy execution" to a sufficient degree, given the importance that respondents attach to these practices. However, higher-performing organizations use these practices to a higher degree than their lower-performing counterparts.

In what could be a related finding, the survey discovered that organizations that have the same CEO for over five years say they're better at strategy execution than organizations with less seasoned leaders. An analysis of the survey's Strategy Execution Index shows the same trend. Therefore, it appears that stable leadership is linked to strategy execution, an important finding at a time when CEO "churn" rates are at record highs. An alternate interpretation of the data is that leaders who are good at execution are more likely to retain the top job over long periods of time.

The single greatest barrier to strategy execution, the survey found, is a lack of adequate resources. Not only does the proper allocation of resources increase a strategy's chances of success, it's a clear sign from leadership that the strategy is viewed as a high corporate priority.

Of course, every organization has different execution challenges. The AMA/HRI survey suggests, however, that mastering certain basics such as clarity, alignment, leadership, adaptability, and resources goes a long way toward enabling companies to turn their best strategic plans into organizational successes.

"The Keys to Strategy Execution" survey summary is available at www.amanet.org/research

> *About AMA*: American Management Association is a world leader in professional development and performance-based learning solutions. AMA provides individuals and organizations worldwide with the knowledge, skills, and tools to achieve performance excellence, adapt to changing realities, and prosper in a complex and competitive world. Each year, thousands of customers learn new skills and behaviors, gain more confidence, advance their careers and contribute to the success of their organizations. AMA offers a range of unique seminars, workshops, conferences, customized corporate programs, online learning, newsletters, journals, and AMA books. Visit online at www.amanet.org.
>
> *About HRI*: For over 30 years, the Human Resource Institute (HRI) has remained dedicated to providing world-class research in the area of people management issues, trends, and practices. Founded in 1969 at the University of Michigan's Institute for Social Research by Dr. William Pyle in collaboration with Dr. Rensis Likert and Dr. George Odiorne, HRI is currently affiliated with the University of Tampa and is widely recognized as one of the top five institutes of its kind in the United States. HRI provides its

members with accurate and timely research that helps facilitate a better understanding of all the people management issues that member organizations face today as well as the trends that are shaping the future. Currently, HRI is following approximately 150 demographic, social, economic, technological, political, legal, and management trends, and there are over 100 major corporations supporting this research with annual grants.

The Peter Principle

The Peter Principle is a theory articulated by Canadian education professor Laurence J. Peter (working from the University of British Columbia and the University of Southern California) in a best-selling book, *The Peter Principle: Why Things Will Always Go Wrong* (1969). The central theme is that "in a hierarchy, every employee tends to rise to his level of incompetence." Accordingly, real work is only accomplished by those who have not yet reached their personal level of incompetence. As a result, slow growth or no growth organizations are much more likely to have incompetent people at many levels than growing companies that are adding people and positions and that can evade realization of the Peter Principle as long as growth continues.

The Peter Principle maintains that in a business, people are promoted to new positions based on how well they perform in their existing position, and not necessarily on whether they already have the skills to succeed at the new position. If they are competent in that new role they will proceed up the ranks to another higher level position. Especially in companies with many layers of management there is an inherent presumption that the employee will be able to do "that little bit more" required at the next level to succeed. According to the Peter Principle the employee will continue to rise until they reach their personal level of incompetence, and will not be promoted further. Provided that their level of incompetence is not gross, they will not be fired from the organization but at the same time will not see additional career growth, leaving the incompetent person in place in the position. Indeed, according to Dr. Peter, as long as incompetence does not threaten the hierarchy, it is usually tolerated by the system. But "supercompetence frequently leads to dismissal because it disrupts the hierarchy. That is why it is more objectionable than impotence within an organization. Ordinary incompetence is a bar to promotion, but is not a cause for firing."

Research has shown that a person who rises to his/her level of incompetence often does not have trouble with their learned skills, but rather with the new skills that they must acquire and use. For example, consider an engineer who has been responsible for managing throughput on a production line. As she rises through the organization she has the engineering skills and experience to manage more lines and even the production of other products. But when she becomes Head of Operations she might need other non-engineering skills such as negotiation and finance. If she lacks those skills or is unable to acquire them directly or indirectly, she becomes a victim of the Peter Principle, locked in the level of her own incompetence.

The Peter Principle is not a hard and fast rule, and companies work to overcome the Peter Principle tendencies. For example, human resources departments work to identify the skill sets required for positions within an organization. Ideally, before a person advances into a new role, he or she is provided with opportunities to acquire the new skills necessary to succeed. Other firms offer mentoring programs so that higher level employees who have achieved in those positions can assist those on the rise to understand the skills that will be necessary as they progress in the organization.

In recent years, the Peter Principle has been supplemented by the *Dilbert* Principle, based on the popular comic strip by Scott Adams. In essence the *Dilbert Principle* suggests that the incompetent rather than the competent are moved into managerial roles, where they are likely to do the least amount of damage to the company. While it is commonly accepted that sub-par employees are shuffled around in an organization, few accept this principle's overall application in the workplace.

See also: Dilbert; Intellectual Capital; Managerial Grid

Further Reading

The Dilbert Principle: A Cubicle's-Eye View of Bosses, Meetings, Management Fads & Other Workplace Afflictions, by Scott Adams, Collins (June 4, 1997).

The Peter Principle, by Laurence J. Peter, Buccaneer Books (February 1993).

"Raising CEO Longevity," a blog posted on September 19, 2007 on www.brandingstrategyinsider.com

Peters, Tom

Tom Peters is considered an expert on business management practices and has been featured in nearly every well-known business magazine. His ideas regarding the value of people in the success of a business revolutionized the way businesses treated such "soft" issues as personnel in relation to "hard" issues like financials and business strategy.

At least two biographies have been written about him and he remains a business icon for many academics, intellectuals, and business professionals around the globe. Born in 1942 in Baltimore, Maryland, Peters studied engineering at Cornell before getting an MBA and PhD from Stanford University. He served in the U.S. Navy and worked in the White House before jointing McKinsey in the mid-1970s as a consultant. He left McKinsey in 1981 to found what is now known as the Tom Peters Group, which includes a consulting business and manages his speaking engagements. Tom Peters now resides in Vermont with his wife Susan.

In their popular management book *In Search of Excellence,* which was first published in 1982, Tom Peters and Robert Waterman argued that there were eight common themes that could explain the difference between highly successful companies and their average peers or competitors. *In Search of Excellence* continues to experience tremendous popularity and remains a widely read business book. It was also the first management book to hit the best-seller list and paved the way for a long line of management experts turned guru to grace the list of best-selling titles.

The eight themes from *In Search of Excellence* are:

1. A bias for action
2. Close to the customer
3. Autonomy and entrepreneurship
4. Productivity through people
5. Hands-on, value-driven ("walk the talk")
6. Stick to the knitting (also known as focus on the core business)
7. Simple form, lean staff
8. Simultaneous loose-tight properties

At the time they published their seminal work, Peters and Waterman were consultants in the San Francisco office of McKinsey, one of the best known strategy consulting firms in the world. The book grew out of a McKinsey research project on the issues of organization, people, and structure. The early research from the project was shared with some of Mc-Kinsey's larger U.S. and global clients and received a great deal of interest.

The findings in their book are founded on the original McKinsey 7-S model, which argues that the *fit* between seven key elements of a business are critical to its success: structure, strategy, and systems (often considered the hard issues), plus style of management, skills, staff, and shared values (often considered the soft issues). The model is designed to identify the interconnectedness of the 7-S's. Although the "harder" issues are easier to change and influence (being more tangible, like computer systems and organizational hierarchies), failure to take into account the "soft" issues (such as the frustration of the staff as they try to use the computer system, or the reaction of management to such frustration) can cause a company to become an average performer or even fail.

The book was a pioneer in demonstrating the value of people in the success of any business. This was contrary to much of the research and literature up to that point, which advocated for a more traditional financials-oriented perspective on businesses. Peters claimed that these "soft" issues were in fact hard ones that had been overlooked by traditional business experts and observers.

Books by Tom Peters: *In Search of Excellence* (co-written with Robert H. Waterman, Jr., 1982); *A Passion for Excellence* (co-written with Nancy Austin, 1985); *Thriving on Chaos* (1987); *Liberation Management* (1992); *The Tom Peters Seminar: Crazy Times Call for Crazy Organizations* (1993); *The Pursuit of WOW!* (1994); *The Circle of Innovation: You Can't Shrink Your Way to Greatness* (1997); *The Brand You50, The Project50 and The Professional Service Firm50* (1999); *Re-imagine! Business Excellence in a Disruptive Age* (2003).

See also: Benchmarking; Competitive Advantage; Empowerment; General Electric (GE) Workout; Herman Miller Furniture; Learning Organization; Performance Management/Performance Measurement; 360-Degree Feedback

Further Reading

www.tompeters.com

Portfolio Career

Why pick one job for your entire life when your interests are likely to change over time? Would not the ideal situation be one in which you could choose a job to fit your current interests? Or would this lead you to a destitute old age, truly skilled in no one thing, a master of nothing at all?

A "portfolio career" is a career path including many different jobs and job functions. It was first defined in the 1980s by Charles Handy, who suggested that rather than choosing an occupation and staying with it through their working careers, people would undertake a portfolio of careers, changing jobs, functions, etc. as their interests changed. There have been many books and articles on the subject since, and it remains at least a moderately popular idea. For instance, *The Guardian* ("Graduate: Mix and Match: Why Pick Just One Job When You Could Have Two, or Three?," November 4, 2006) noted,

> The arguments for pursuing a portfolio career at the beginning of one's adult life are clear. Harvard psychology professor Daniel Gilbert, author of bestseller, *Stumbling on Happiness*, believes the best way to figure out what will make you happy is to try it. A portfolio career gives you the opportunity to try three or four types of work at the same time, and to keep switching choices until you come up with a portfolio you like.

Yet there are concerns about a portfolio career approach. One is that individuals might become a "jack of all trades" but a "master of none," and with it lack the specialized knowledge it takes to succeed in certain disciplines. Others note that a portfolio career might be of genuine interest, but financing one can be difficult, as most people would constantly start at entry-level positions that are generally not well paid.

Businesses may not be particularly keen on the idea, either. Other than in jobs in which a high turnover rate is expected (e.g., retail or fast-food jobs), an organization invests a lot in training an employee to do the work required. This investment is lost if the employee becomes bored and moves on. On the other hand, perhaps some businesses will move to hiring

Why I Do This: Limo Driver, NREMT-P
(Nationally Registered Emergency Medical Technician, Paramedic)
Chris is also a full-time firefighter/paramedic.

Chris Greim

When I'm not at the fire station, I have been working for the past three years as a limo driver. As elegant as that sounds we do so much more than just drive limos. I have driven six, eight, ten, and fourteen passenger vehicles. Also I drive fifteen passenger vans, and several Lincoln Sedans. My job varies from transporting people to and from their homes to and from several local airports. We take people "out" for the night, concerts, ball games, weddings, bachelor/bachelorette parties, and proms just to name a few. I have driven as far away as 350 miles to Pennsylvania and most recently about 250 miles to New York City. Yes the job definitely has some great benefits and it can be quite glitzy.

It's hard to describe in a short period of time why I like my job but I have to say I absolutely love it. First when you have people in the limo they are usually there because they want to be and therefore I find that I am dealing with very happy people. I enjoy people. There is so much to be learned from people if you just listen. Another aspect of the job I enjoy, listening. You get people, who are going on vacation or business trips, and they sometimes talk and sometimes they are very engrossed in their business. When people take a limo to go out you never know where you may end up. Sometimes it's out for dinner, maybe a concert, or a late night run to the casino. Either way you need to be flexible and always have a smile on your face.

I have to say that as much fun and enjoyment I get out of seeing people happy for whatever reason they take a limo, there is nothing as gratifying as the look on young teenagers faces as a shiny black or white limousine pulling into their driveways for the prom. For most it's their first time ever in a limo and they are so excited anyway. I always give the prom goers a little extra attention and really roll out the red carpet. For all the fun and excitement there is in a limo, sometimes you are just picking people up from the airport and that's ok too.

No matter what the job is or where it takes me I always look forward to going to work. I never know exactly where I may end up. Typically I will go in the morning and sometimes be there all day. Sometimes it's one airport trip sometimes it's a wedding that begins in the morning and winds up very late that night dropping off the newly weds as they head off for their honeymoon. My job is to transport my customers from point A to point B and everywhere in between, safely, and with courtesy. Yes I have had celebrities, and yes the tips are great. But the bottom line is I love what I do. It's fun and satisfying. If someone needs a ride and I can provide them with a little pampering and a smile I feel my job is complete.

contract workers when possible, thus avoiding most of the costs of training and also avoiding payment of benefits, various taxes, and other expenses.

Still, to the individual, the idea of following one's dreams, wherever they might lead and in whatever direction they might flow, is appealing, if not always practical.

Charles Handy

Charles Handy is, as *The Economist* (May 26, 2006) describes, "the wise old man of British management, an avuncular figure with a keen ear for a memorable metaphor. His books have titles like *The Empty Raincoat* and *The Elephant and the Flea,* and he talks of phenomena such as "the shamrock organisation" (companies with three levels of employment: full-time workers; subcontractors/outsourcers; and part-time specialists) and "the portfolio worker (people who have a number of 'jobs, clients and types of work' simultaneously)."

Like the titles of his books, Charles Handy has an interesting background. Handy was the son of a Protestant Irish vicar, went to Oxford and worked in remote locations for Shell Oil before attending MIT and working as a professor at the London Business School. Today, he is a self-described social-philosopher.

Works by Charles Handy: *Understanding Organizations* (London: Penguin, 1976); *The Future of Work* (Oxford: Basil Blackwell, 1984); *Gods of Management* (London: Business Books, 1986); *The Making of Managers* (London: Longman, 1988); *The Age of Unreason* (London: Business Books, 1989); *The Empty Raincoat* (London: Hutchinson, 1994); *The Hungry Spirit* (London: Hutchinson, 1997).

See also: Free Agent; Lifetime Employment; Mid-Career

Further Reading

Building Your Career Portfolio, by Carol A. Poore, Cengage Delmar Learning, 1st ed. (May 1, 2001).
"When Many Careers are Better than One," by Randy Ray, special to the *Globe and Mail*, posted on www.theglobeandmail.com on May 9, 2007.

PowerPoint

PowerPoint is the presentation software package produced by Microsoft. Part of the Microsoft Office Suite, it is intended to help its users prepare presentations for work, school, or other uses. In the same way that the Word program helps with word processing and Excel with spreadsheets, PowerPoint helps its users organize and present their thoughts clearly and concisely for presentations. Although not the early market leader in the presentation software space (that was held by Harvard Graphics), Power-Point rose to prominence with the increasing popularity of the Microsoft Office software suite. With a foundation in business, the use of Power-Point spread to associations, groups, and schools.

Early features of PowerPoint incorporated graphics and build-ins that allowed users to build up individual data points to create a final slide that summarized key points. Such a building-block approach was designed to help users build their arguments as the data on the slide concurrently filled up. Other features were standardized templates for presentations and op-portunities for inserting company logos and other items that made the presentation feel like it was part of the fabric of the organization.

With updates to Microsoft Office, there have been steady changes to the PowerPoint software program. A new release in 2007 promised increased security and opportunities for collaboration among users, including a rede-signed interface; reuse of content through slide libraries; features allowing the user to manage, track, and review presentations more easily; and an increased ability to share presentations by converting them to other file formats.

While there are an estimated thirty million PowerPoint presentations given every day, and the tool has proven its usefulness, there are many who are less then enthused about listening to another PowerPoint presentation. Expressions such as "mind-numbing" are common, and for some Power-Point presentations have become a proxy for hard-driving business.

Indeed the backlash against PowerPoint has created phrases such as "death by PowerPoint" and even a book by the same name, as well as more instructional texts such as *Solving the PowerPoint Predicament: Using Digital Media for Effective Communication*. A running joke is that those that complain about PowerPoint will give you a PowerPoint slide with bullets of their pet peeves about the program and its use.

Despite criticisms of PowerPoint, it legitimately offers benefits. If used well, it can add life to lifeless presentations, it can keep the presenter on message, and it can be a helpful aid. For example, if a presenter freezes in front of an audience they are often able to get going by reading off the first line of the first slide. Suggestions about how to improve PowerPoint presentations are as much for the person presenting as for the actual presentation. They include:

- Don't read from the slides verbatim. Presumably the audience is able to read for themselves and the presenter should be using the points as a starting point for a deeper discussion.
- Don't overload the slides with material. More text in a smaller sized font just creates tired eyes, not a more informed audience.
- Don't overdo artwork and effects so that these tools detract rather than enhance the flow and delivery of the presentation.
- If multiple people are presenting, collect all the presentations on a single machine so as to minimize interruptions associated with plugging and unplugging gear. Do think about the audience and the message that you want to communicate rather than immediately launching into bullet point sound bites.

By following common sense and keeping the audience in mind, PowerPoint presentations can be an effective way to organize communication. However, one needs to recognize that PowerPoint is but a tool. If the presentation is a flop, the root of the problem is with the presenter or his/her material, rather than the tool itself.

See also: Training and Development

Further Reading

Teach Yourself PowerPoint 2007, by Moira Stephen, McGraw-Hill, 4th ed. (July 23, 2007).

Real Time

The term real time comes from its use in original simulation exercises—exercises, either virtual or real, simulating an event or series of events—and has primarily been used in business as a reference to computing and computer science. Originally real time referred to a simulation that matched the rate of the real process it was simulating and that was no slower nor any faster than that process. It is often used to mean the time required for a computer to solve a problem, measured from the time data are fed to the program to the time a solution is received.

In today's information intense environment, real time is used to describe instant access to current information with no delay in time, such as real time stock, options, bondd or futures quotes on the Internet or real time video conferencing. In both cases, there are tremendous advantages to having real time communications. In the case of stock, options, bond, or futures quotes, since prices change constantly, someone who is buying or selling will want to have access to accurate and current information when deciding whether and when to execute a trade. In the case of videoconferencing, the tool would not serve its purpose if participants could not communicate with each other as though they were in the same room.

An event that happens in real time happens essentially at the same moment, and both the sender and receiver have access to the event or transmission of information. For example, when you chat in a chat room or send an instant message, you are interacting in real time. On the other hand, when you send or receive an e-mail message, that communication is not occurring in real time, as there is some delay between when the sender sends the message and when the receiver reads and responds to the message.

Other examples of real time computer systems that are critical for safety and/or production requirements include: antilock brakes, which respond immediately to changes in road conditions to benefit the driver; manufacturing and industrial robots, which respond quickly to keep assembly and production lines moving at full speed; and space flight computers, which

---

Why I Do This: Librarian
Sheila Putnam

The stereotypical librarian with thick glasses, severely styled hair, and orthopedic shoes went out with the dinosaurs. Librarians today are multi-talented, cutting-edge technicians who handle a tremendous variety of needs and requests.

There's no typical day in a library because every patron's situation is unique. Over the course of a week I read to little kids; make creative displays; help folks with copying, faxing, scanning and Internet searching; choose books to buy; process materials; recommend movies; sell goods; and talk to lots of interesting people.

I started out as a volunteer and learned on the job. Good people skills, attention to detail, and the willingness to learn new skills are important qualifications. But the biggest thing is to love reading!

---

respond to changing conditions in order to keep the rocket ship on course. Many vehicles come standard with Global Positioning System (GPS) devices, which provide real time information on driving directions between a vehicle's current location and the desired destination. While GPS devices are not routinely considered safety features, they can serve to provide peace of mind and even safety for many drivers.

Examples of systems that are not typically real time include banking back office functions, human resource management systems, and order tracking systems. While you can go on line and track a package that you ordered via the Internet, it is unlikely that you can observe your package en route to you. You can find the last place it was handled, but not the current street location of the truck that is carrying your package. That said, as information technology and computing become more sophisticated and the consumer demand increases for real time systems across supply and distribution chains, many enterprises have implemented real time systems in these areas as well. And enterprises have found that these systems can provide both significant cost savings and in some cases competitive differentiation from others in their industry or market space.

See also: E-mail; Intranet/Extranet; Networking; 24/7; Virtual Teams

Further Reading

Real-Time Strategic Change, by Robert W. Jacobs, Berrett-Koehler Publishers, New Ed ed. (January 15, 1997).

Reengineering

Reengineering, also referred to as Business Process Reengineering (BPR), Business Process Redesign, Business Transformation, and Process Change Management, is a management approach that is intended to examine the underlying processes that support a business and improve their efficiency. Most often this involves eliminating as much as possible any non-value adding activities and tasks. Reengineering essentially means doing things differently and involves fundamentally changing the way an enterprise or organization conducts business to align their underlying business processes and workflow with their business strategy.

Instead of organizing an enterprise into functional areas (such as finance, marketing, operations, sales, etc.) and looking at the tasks performed by each of those functions, according to reengineering theory, enterprises should organize around a series of processes that often cross functional boundaries and even enterprise boundaries (such as suppliers, distributors, customers, and other business partners). This may involve creating new processes that span supply and distribution chains across organizations, including materials acquisition, production, marketing, and distribution.

Reengineering became popular in business culture in the early 1990s when Michael Hammer and James Champy published a series of books including *Reengineering the Corporation, Reengineering Management,* and *The Agenda.* The premise of Hammer and Champy's work on reengineering is that by examining the business objectives of the organization and redesigning the workflow and business processes from the "ground up" to align with its business objectives, an organization can achieve increased productivity, improved performance, greater cost savings, and superior customer service. The ultimate goal of reengineering, according to the authors, is to create competitive advantage for an organization. Rather than consuming valuable time and resources passing tasks from one functional area of an organization to another, proponents of reengineering theory argue that an organization can generate greater value by creating processes that span these functions and are designed to deliver the product or services more efficiently.

Reengineering involves applying the resources of an organization, namely the people, technology, and processes, in a more rational way in order to better support business strategies and objectives in today's environment. While not essential, the use of information technology to improve performance and reduce cost is often integral to the reengineering process. A redesign of processes is followed by the application of appropriate technology to support the newly designed workflow and processes.

Implementation of reengineering theory led to several other developments in leading management practices, including the use of cross-functional teams, customer relationship management (CRM), enterprise resource planning (ERP), and supply chain management.

Throughout the 1990s enterprises were eager to benefit from the financial advantages promised by the reengineering movement. While reengineering differs from earlier and later forms of cost reduction efforts in that it is intended to be customer and business strategy oriented, by the mid-1990s reengineering had earned a bad reputation as many reengineering projects in practice resulted in significant workforce reductions.

Critics of reengineering often note that one of its pitfalls is that the enterprise becomes so focused on internal issues that it fails to identify areas of competitive differentiation and competitive advantage, such as new products or services or radical changes in the marketplace. In one classic example, American Express spent considerable time and resources to reengineer its credit card business. In isolation, the work at American Express might have been considered a success. On the other hand, while American Express was reengineering, Visa and Master Card, its competitors, introduced a new product known today as the corporate procurement card that generated far greater economic benefits than American Express's reengineering work. It took American Express more than a year to catch up with its competitors in the corporate procurement business.

Other critics argue that the value of reengineering as a way to produce sustainable competitive advantage is limited, as reengineering efforts can easily be copied by competitors and are therefore not sustainable. Add to this the costs in time, money, and corporate focus, and reengineering loses much of its glow. If done well, reengineering may bring about a radical improvement, but a business must be absolutely sure that this process is the best solution for its needs.

See also: Change Agent/Change Management; Crisis/Risk Management; Mission Statement; Performance Management/Performance Measurement

Further Reading

Built to Last: Successful Habits of Visionary Companies, by Jim Collins and Jerry I. Porras, Collins (November 2, 2004).

Reengineering the Corporation: A Manifesto for Business Revolution, by Michael Hammer and James Champy, Collins Business Essentials (December 2003).

Relationship Marketing

The American Marketing Association defines relationship marketing as "Marketing with the conscious aim to develop and manage long-term and/or trusting relationships with customers, distributors, suppliers, or other parties in the marketing environment."

So what does that really mean for a business? Often a business will have two different types of customers. The first is transactional customers—customers that will buy your product once, provide only a modest or one-time contribution to your profits, and may or may not purchase from you again. By contrast, relationship customers purchase frequently, often in large quantities, and generally will have an ongoing need for your product. Clearly you want to have a relationship with the latter group of customers and be in a position to influence their purchase decisions. At times, marketers think of transactional customers as the target in consumer marketing and relationship customers as the target in business-to-business marketing—though that is not always the case.

As a result companies use different tactics in marketing to relationship and transactional customers. There are fewer relationship customers and therefore businesses will have a sales force targeted directly to their relationship accounts. The sales force will attempt to meet and even anticipate the needs for the customer for sales and service. Moreover, effective relationship marketing will work to capture the lifetime value of that customer. Building a relationship with a customer takes time, and by nurturing the customer relationship the company can receive a constant and increasing flow of orders.

Dell is an example of a company that effectively used relationship marketing to establish its business, using relationship marketing techniques to penetrate 25 percent of the Fortune 500 companies (Dell Online, Case # 598–116, Harvard Business Publishing, 1999). V. Kasturi Rangan noted in *Transforming Your Go-To-Market Strategy: Three Principles of Channel Stewardship* (Harvard Business School Press, 2006)

Dell segmented its customers along two dimensions. The first was by demographics: customer size, industry (such as education or government), and so on. The second dimension was customer buying behavior: either relationship or transaction. Relationship customers bought in large quantities on an ongoing basis. They sought standardized product features that were compatible with their installed base. For these reasons, price was an important buying criterion for relationship customers. On the other hand, transaction customers—mainly small and medium-sized businesses—viewed each purchase as a one-time occasion and emphasized up-to-date product features more than price.

Each segment had different demand-chain needs and also represented differing revenue potential. Dell created a sales model (part of Dell's supply-chain capability) with a differing cost to serve based on profit potential. Relationship customers bought through Dell sales representatives. The largest customers had dedicated teams, including program managers and technical support as well as sales personnel. By contrast, the transaction customer sales force was almost exclusively telephone based. Customers called Dell and received knowledgeable support from telephone sales reps. By combining buying behavior and segmentation based on size and industry, Dell was able to sense and respond to the distinct demand-chain needs of fine-grained segments.

Starting in the late 1990s companies began to use technology to help them better execute relationship marketing strategies to existing customers and build relationships with customers too small to reach effectively without technology. While there are many such productivity tools, the most visible is Customer Relationship Management (CRM). The market leader in CRM was Siebel Systems, who pioneered the market space. (Seibel was subsequently purchased by Oracle.) The Siebel CRM system sought to provide technical support for all the business processes that touch a customer, including billing and delivery, and included applications for sales force automation, sales order entry, sales and customer history, and product configuration.

Regardless of—or perhaps because of—the technology used, relationship marketing is still an important part of business today, enabling businesses to better reach potential long-term customers and keep on top of those customers' needs. In a business environment with finite numbers of long-term customers, a company continually needs to demonstrate its ability to market effectively to this important customer base.

See also: Best Practice; Competitive Advantage; Intangibles; Mass Customization

Further Reading

Masters of Sales, by Ivan R. Misner and Don Morgan, Entrepreneur Press, 1st ed. (August 15, 2007).

S

Sarbanes–Oxley Act of 2002

In recent years, there have been several large-scale corporate accounting scandals in the United States. Enron, WorldCom, and Tyco International, among others, have made headlines due to the enrichment of their executive management teams through insider trading and questionable accounting practices.

These practices, while enriching upper management, were almost always at the expense of employees and shareholders. Billions of dollars were lost as employee retirement plans dissolved away and shareholder investments became worthless. These huge losses shook the financial markets, resulting in investor mistrust and uncertainty.

In July 2002, in reaction to these highly publicized scandals, Senator Paul Sarbanes (D-MD) and Representative Michael Oxley (R-OH) drafted legislation designed to improve the accuracy and reliability of financial disclosures.

This legislation, known as the Sarbanes–Oxley Act of 2002 (Pub. L. No. 107–204, 116 Stat. 745), was overwhelmingly approved by both houses of Congress; it passed the House by a vote of 423–3 and by the Senate 99–0. The Sarbanes–Oxley Act mandates a wide-sweeping accounting framework for all public companies doing business in the United States. The Sarbanes–Oxley Act is now considered to be the most significant legislation affecting United States securities laws since the New Deal in the 1930s.

On July 30, 2002, President George W. Bush signed the Act into law. Upon signing it, he commented:

And today I sign the most far-reaching reforms of American business practices since the time of Franklin Delano Roosevelt. This new law sends very clear messages that all concerned must heed. This law says to every dishonest corporate leader: you will be exposed and punished; the era of low standards and false profits is over; no boardroom in America is above or beyond the law.

This law says to honest corporate leaders: your integrity will be recognized and rewarded, because the shadow of suspicion will be lifted from good companies that respect the rules.

This law says to corporate accountants: the high standards of your profession will be enforced without exception; the auditors will be audited; the accountants will be held to account.

This law says to shareholders that the financial information you receive from a company will be true and reliable, for those who deliberately sign their names to deception will be punished.

This law says to workers: we will not tolerate reckless practices that artificially drive up stock prices and eventually destroy the companies, and the pensions, and your jobs.

And this law says to every American: there will not be a different ethical standard for corporate America than the standard that applies to everyone else. The honesty you expect in your small businesses, or in your workplaces, in your community or in your home, will be expected and enforced in every corporate suite in this country . . . .

Corporate misdeeds will be found and will be punished. This law authorizes new funding for investigators and technology at the Securities and Exchange Commission to uncover wrongdoing. The SEC will now have the administrative authority to bar dishonest directors and officers from ever again serving in positions of corporate responsibility. The penalties for obstructing justice and shredding documents are greatly increased. Corporate crime will no longer pay. CEOs who profit by betraying the public trust will be forced to return those gains to investors. And the maximum prison term for common types of fraud has quadrupled from five to twenty years.

Major provisions of Sarbanes–Oxley include:

- The establishment of the *Public Company Accounting Oversight Board*, a private, nonprofit corporation whose primary duty is to ensure that financial statements are audited according to independent standards.
- A regulation that companies must evaluate and disclose the effectiveness of their financial internal controls and that independent auditors must confirm such disclosure.
- Chief Executive Officers and Chief Financial Officers must sign off on their company's financial reports.

- A requirement that companies establish fully independent audit committees, whose responsibility is to oversee the relationship between the company and its auditor.
- Prohibitions against personal loans to any executive officer or director
- Detailed restrictions on insider trading
- Stiffer penalties for violations of securities law
- Protections for employee *whistleblowers*

While most support the aims of the Sarbanes–Oxley legislation, its application has received mixed reviews. For some, "Sox," unlike the Boston Red Sox, is a burden that many would like to see scaled-back. Indeed the checking of internal controls inherent in Sarbanes–Oxley is such that some critics suggest that the law damages U.S. business competitiveness, with estimates suggesting that $6 billion was spent in 2006 alone in complying with Sarbanes–Oxley, with the financial burden especially onerous for some 6 million publicly-traded small businesses. In September 2006, *The Economist* noted, "Americans and foreign firms alike see Sarbanes–Oxley which was passed in the wake of the Enron scandal as intrusive, expensive, and heavy-handed." However, in a *Fortune* magazine article, Paul Sarbanes responded to the criticism, noting, "These people have already forgotten what happened at Enron and Worldcom. . . . The bill is about ensuring that public companies have a legitimate system of financial controls. To me that is a worthwhile cost."

See also: Code of Ethics; Enron; Whistleblower

Further Reading

The Complete Guides to Sarbanes-Oxley: Understanding How Sarbanes-Oxley Affects Your Business, by Stephen M. Bainbridge, Adams Business (2007).

"Stop Whining About SarbOx!" by Andy Serwer, *Fortune*, New York: Aug 7, 2006, Issue 3, page 39.

What is Sarbanes-Oxley? by Guy Lander, McGraw Hill (November 2003).

http://thecaq.aicpa.org/ (The Center for Audit Quality)

Scenario Planning

Have you ever wondered "*what if*," followed by a hypothetical series of events? Almost everyone has thought about future events in this way. "What if I don't get in to my first choice college?" or "What if I flunk my math test?" are examples of future hypothetical events.

In scenario planning, multiple "scenarios" or contingency plans are developed to address such *what ifs* should they become a reality. For example, what are some different scenarios that might result if you were not accepted at your first choice college? You might:

- attend another college that accepted you, and transfer after a year;
- attend another college that accepted you, and decide that you like it;
- decide to work for a year and reapply to your first choice.

Businesses have adopted scenario planning as a way of being prepared for different future contingencies. Scenario planning is a proactive way to think and plan for future developments, instead of simply being passive as change occurs.

Scenario planning was first developed by the Rand Corporation for military use following World War II. The U.S. Air Force tried to predict what its enemies might do, so they could prepare different response strategies.

Businesses began to adopt scenario planning as a discipline in the early 1970s. Royal Dutch Shell pioneered work in this area. Shell wanted to understand the numerous external events and factors that were likely to affect the price of oil in the United States, factors that were not under the direct control of Shell.

At the time, numerous events were unfolding in the energy sector:

- Oil reserves in the United States were slowly depleting;
- American demand for oil was steadily increasing;
- OPEC countries were organizing, developing into a cartel. Most of the countries in OPEC were Islamic, and they resented Western support of Israel in the 1967 six-day war.

Shell developed numerous scenarios to account for any significant change in these factors. The outcome of this process was the development of contingency plans should any of these key factors transpire or change

Why I Do This: Home Care Provider; Dental Assistant, Correctional Facility; Animal Caretaker

Lisa Dell Bonney

I do a number of things because I'm raising two children, and I like the daily variety. These jobs fit into my schedule, and the way I want to live.

My "main" job is being a home health care provider. I take care of a woman who is fifty-three years old. She was in a terrible car accident when she was eighteen, and since then, she needs twenty-four-hour care. She can't walk; she's blind; and she can do very little for herself. I enjoy taking care of her, and listening to what she says, and how she responds to the things that I say. A lot of people are scared of people who are this incapacitated. If you were to meet her, you might say, "How do you take care of her?" But I relate to her very well. I do four-hour shifts with her, and I also do night shifts—from 7 P.M. through 8 A.M. the next day.

I found this job in the help wanted section of the newspaper. I didn't have any experience in the field. You might like this kind of work if you're a compassionate person, and you don't mind helping people keep themselves clean and taken care of, in the most basic of ways. It doesn't sound as if you could find satisfaction in doing this, but you really can. It shows you what's important in life; if you're having a bad day and you go to work, you realize pretty quickly, "Hey, it's not a bad day, really."

One of my other jobs is assisting the dentist at the county house of corrections. The jail. There's a room set up like a dentist's office, and the inmates have appointments, and come in, just as you would go to the dentist. I hand the dentist the instruments; I sterilize the equipment; I prep for various procedures; and I make sure that all of the equipment is accounted for. The inmates are incarcerated for reasons ranging from passing bad checks, to murder. I found this job in the local paper, too. I didn't have any experience. They taught me on the job. I enjoy talking to the inmates. They don't see many people who aren't either prisoners or correctional officers, so they tend to want to talk, which is fine.

Finally, I take care of a number of dogs and horses for their owners. That's a natural job for me; I love animals. I got these jobs through word of mouth. Some of them are only for a weekend; some are for a week or more.

in the future. Shell also recognized that the environment in which it operated was constantly changing, requiring updates to scenarios on a frequent basis.

In a corporation, each key discipline—new product development, marketing, finance, human resources, etc.—is subject to external influences. These influences might be economic, political, technological, environmental, or demographic areas, to name just a few. In companies using scenario planning, it is common for each discipline to develop its own scenario planning to account for these outside contingencies.

The Scenario Planning Process

Scenario planning is a collaborative, conversation-led process, which enables the integration of a wide array of ideas. There are sequential steps, resulting in the formulation of contingency planning for an array of future events that may confront the company. Scenario planning is not the same thing as forecasting, which relies on a linear projection of past events into the future. Scenarios are not built via consensus, but rather respect, and accommodate different points of view.

Generally, scenario planning follows this sequence:

- Identify the specific issue or decision under discussion. For example, a company may be in the process of deciding whether or not to acquire another company, or branch into new areas for product development, or where to locate a new factory.
- Decide on a timeframe for the future, and the degree of uncertainty of your scenarios. The degree of uncertainty is higher the more years out you go; scenarios that project out to twenty years have higher degrees of uncertainty than do scenarios looking two years out.
- Specify all the external forces that might affect the company, the industry segment, etc.
- Select the two or three most important of these external forces. Develop multiple scenarios representing.
- The current situation as it now stands (baseline).
- If external influence A were to dominate.
- If external situation B were to dominate.
- Hypothesize how other key players might behave under each scenario. Key players may include government regulators, customers, suppliers, competitors, etc.
- Examine each scenario to identify potential opportunities and/or threats.

At the end of this process, the company is in a position to develop an action plan for each scenario, thus being in a far better position than if it simply reacted to change. If management disseminates these scenarios and contingency plans throughout the organization, it is far easier for employees to band together and implement required action, since they already have a roadmap approved by their management.

See also: Benchmarking; Budget; Change Agent/Change Management; Competitive Advantage; Crisis/Risk Management; Entrepreneur; Mission Statement

Further Reading

Scenario Planning Handbook: Developing Strategies in Uncertain Times, by Ian Wilson, and Bill Ralston, South-Western Educational Pub., 1st ed. (June 9, 2006).

Scenario Planning: The Link Between Future and Strategy, by Mats Lindgren, and Hans Bandhold, Palgrave Macmillan (February 22, 2003).

"Three Decades of Scenario Planning in Shell," by Peter Cornelius, Alexander Van de Putte, and Mattia Romani, *California Management Review.* Berkeley: Fall 2005. Vol. 48, Issue 1; pg. 92.

www.valuebasedmanagement.net

Shareholder Value

Shareholder value is the value returned to shareholders (owners) of a business. From the perspective of the balance sheet, shareholder value is a simple calculation: assets less liabilities equals shareholder value. Despite simplicity of calculation the concept of shareholder value is complex.

In its purest form, the managers of a company stand in place of the shareholders. More formally they have a fiduciary responsibility to the shareholders—a responsibility to act in the shareholders' best interests. In an ideal state, this means growing the company and increasing profitability, and with it returns to the shareholders. This can be accomplished in a variety of ways including new products, new strategies, acquisitions, etc. These traditional strategies can be successful and create increased shareholder value or be "disasters" and destroy shareholder value.

Bad strategy or its execution can lead to dramatic losses in shareholder value. For example, consider what happened to shareholder value at Boston Scientific following an ill-advised purchase of a related company, Guidant in 2006.

Shortly after Boston Scientific [made] a $27 billion acquisition of Guidant in March, the purchase started to look like a horrible mistake. The overall market for Guidant's main product began to fall after growing 20 percent a year. Analysts blamed Guidant: Its string of quality-related product recalls likely caused cardiac patients and their physicians to lose confidence in its brand name. As if that weren't enough, safety concerns cropped up over Boston Scientific's other important product, drug-coated stents. This year the company lost about 40 percent of its shareholder value (*BusinessWeek*, December 18, 2006).

As seen above, in some cases it is clear how management action (or inaction) has a direct effect on shareholder value. In other cases, the linkage is less clear. One such area is corporate social responsibility. One side argues that when a company is being socially responsible it is "doing good" and that will in turn create a positive positioning for the company that will improve its profitability and return to shareholders. This is the idea of "doing well by doing good." On the other side of this argument is that corporate social responsibility cannot be connected to shareholder value and as such that corporations should leave the choice of social giving to individual shareholders.

In May 28, 2005, *The Economist* took on this debate ("The biggest contract—Business and Society") noting that on one side of the current debate is the view that social issues are peripheral to the challenges of corporate management. The sole legitimate purpose of business is to create shareholder value. On the other side are the proponents of corporate social responsibility, who argue that corporations need to go further in mitigating their social impact. The article suggests that a starting point toward a solution might be "for CEOs to articulate publicly the purpose of business in less dry terms than shareholder value. Shareholder value should continue to be seen as the critical measure of business success. However, it may be more accurate, more motivating—and indeed more beneficial to shareholder value over the long term—to describe business's ultimate purpose as the efficient provision of goods and services that society wants."

Given the importance of shareholder value, much has been written on ways that management can increase it. Given criticism that managers often act to increase near term shareholder value (and with it their own salaries) at the expense of long term value, Alfred Rappaport, emeritus professor at Northwestern University, offered "Ten Ways to Create Shareholder Value" (*Harvard Business Review*, September 2006). Among the ten:

1. Do not manage earning or provide earnings guidance
2. Make strategic decisions that maximize the expected value even if they lower near term earnings
3. Make acquisitions that maximize expected value even if they lower near term earnings
4. Carry only assets that maximize value
5. Return cash to shareholders when there are no credible value-creating opportunities to invest in the business

See also: Intangibles; Intellectual Capital; Lean Manufacturing; Mission Statement; Reengineering; Spin-off/Spinout; Stakeholder Theory/Management

Further Reading

Creating Shareholder Value: A Guide for Managers and Investors, by Alfred Rappaport, Free Press, rev. sub. ed. (December 1, 1997).

Shareholder Value: Key To Corporate Development, edited by Christopher J. Clarke, 1st ed., New York: Pergamon Press (1993).

"Ten Things That Destroy Shareholder Value," Stanley Bing, *Fortune*, New York: Jul 24, 2000. Vol. 142, Issue 3; pg. 69.

Six Sigma

As *BusinessWeek* noted in December 2006, many have come to know the Motorola company for its "cool cell phone," but the company's most lasting "claim to fame" is the quality improvement process called Six Sigma. Six Sigma is a quality management process that strives for the development of near-perfect products and services.

The Greek letter "Sigma" stands for a statistical concept that describes how far a given process deviates from perfection. "Six Sigma quality" means that, in a given process, there may not be more than 3.4 defects per million "opportunities" or, in other words, there needs to be nearly

Why I Do This: Senior Consultant in the Health & Benefits Practice Human Resource Consulting Firm
Frank Lawson*

The cost of health care to individuals and companies in the United States has been increasing at double-digit rates for the better part of the last seven years. To combat this rising cost of health care (and to stem these rising costs from cutting into profits), companies have implemented many strategies in attempting to reduce their expenditures on employee health care. These include cost shifting (i.e., company pays less; employee pays more), cutback (or elimination) of health benefits and/or adjustment of coverage for medical benefits and pharmacy benefits. Although all these strategies can and have been used, little attention had been paid to the effect of individual behavior, its impact on one's health and subsequent impact on health care costs. Many companies now are embracing the adoption of Health and Productivity Management solutions as a way to help reduce health care costs for both the employer and employee under the premise that a healthy (or healthier) employee uses less health care.

My job is helping companies to support their employees in maintaining their health and productivity, help them make wise decisions about the use of health care services, and to help limit health-related benefit expenses. I work closely with major corporations, health plans and other provider organizations to develop strategies tailored to the employee and enrollee population.

My day to day job can vary greatly based on the number of clients I'm working with at any given moment in time. I can be working one day with a company that is in the initial stages of developing a health and productivity program for their employees while at the same time working with other companies who are selection vendors to implement their health and productivity management program. It's rare that two companies are at the same place in reference to their internal health care initiatives and I'm working with more than one client at once. Thus my day-to-day job is never consistent.

I like my job because I believe very strongly in improving and/or maintaining one's personal health. Working for Mercer's Health & Productivity specialty practice, I'm working to help companies improve the health and well-being of their employees through the implementation of different care management programs. By providing employees with different tools by which they can maintain and/or improve their health, these companies can actually become more financially sound. I also like my job because no day is the same. I work on various client projects at once. Variety keeps me fresh!!

I think someone who enjoys strategy development and thinking through problems would enjoy this job (and be good at it). I think anyone who is passionate about their personal health and who understands how being healthy improves one's quality of life would also be good in this job.

*Name changed for privacy.

flawless execution of any particular process. For most corporations, Six Sigma is a tool that helps them improve their performance and decrease product flaws, leading to an improvement in product quality, employee morale, and, ultimately, profitability.

Six Sigma uses a defined methodology, based on data and statistical analyses, to measure and improve a company's operational performance, practices, systems, and products. Through this approach, defects are identified and then prevented, thereby anticipating and exceeding the expectations of customers. Increased customer loyalty is the expected result.

The term Six Sigma was coined by a Motorola engineer Bill Smith, and is a registered trademark of Motorola. It is the culmination of much quality management work that preceded it:

- In the nineteenth century, Carl Frederick Gauss developed the statistical concepts of the normal distribution and the least-squares approximation method, on which Six Sigma is based.
- In the 1920s, Walter Shewhart of the Bell Telephone Company used the concept of Six Sigma in his work on quality management. Dr. Shewhart believed that a lack of information greatly hampered the efforts of control and management processes in a production environment.

Dr. Shewhart developed his "Statistical Process Control" as an aid in management decision-making. He demonstrated that three sigma from the mean is the point in a process that required correction.

In the 1980s, Motorola faced serious competition from Japanese manufacturers. One Japanese company acquired a Motorola television factory and produced televisions with one-twentieth the number of defects compared with the Motorola televisions. Motorola's CEO at the time, Bob Galvin, realized that his company must become serious about quality and commissioned his engineers to work on quality improvement.

Upon studying the problem, the engineers realized that the quality standards that were currently in use were insufficient. Measuring defects per thousands of opportunities was not fine enough to affect product quality. Motorola shifted its quality standard to Six Sigma, with the result being a notable improvement in product quality, increased profitability, and large savings from a reduction in waste.

Motorola also developed a "benchmarking" program that assessed the specific level of quality of its own products and those of its competitors. Through this process, many of Motorola's products have achieved "best in class" status. In 1988, Motorola was awarded the much-coveted Malcolm Baldrige Award for Quality.

Other companies adopted Six Sigma early on and have remained committed to the approach over time. General Electric, Raytheon, and Honeywell International were among the early pioneers.

Six Sigma has evolved over the course of its lifetime and has been adopted by dozens of companies. Six Sigma now encompasses not simply metrics, but also a methodology and a management system:

- As a metric (3.4 defects per million opportunities, known as DPMO);
- To improve existing business processes, Six Sigma employs the DMAIC methodology (define opportunity, measure performance, analyze opportunity, improve performance, control performance);
- To develop new products or processes, Six Sigma employs the DMADV process (define, measure, analyze, design, verify).

As a management system, Six Sigma is different from other quality management programs in that it is a top-down solution, designed to help organizations focus on:

- Understanding and managing customer requirements;
- Aligning key business processes and resources to achieve these requirements;
- Employing rigorous data analysis to minimize variation in those processes;
- Developing quick, sustainable improvement to key processes.

Motorola found, through its own mistakes, that Six Sigma only works if its CEO and executives are fully trained and supportive of the methodology. Training of the other employees follows down the hierarchy to the plant worker. This way, managers helped train workers and explain the complex statistical methodology.

There are five key roles within an organization that are necessary for successful Six Sigma implementation:

1. *Executive Leadership* (CEO and other executives) are responsible for determining the focus of Six Sigma implementation. It also provides the other players with the resources needed to explore new ideas for breakthrough improvements.
2. *Champions* are responsible for Six Sigma execution across the organization in an integrated manner. *Champions* are also mentors to *Black Belts.*
3. *Master Black Belts'* sole job responsibility is Six Sigma. They act as in-house expert coaches for the organization.
4. *Black Belts* work under Master Black Belts to apply Six Sigma methodology to specific projects. They devote 100% of their time to Six Sigma.
5. *Green Belts* are responsible for Six Sigma implementation along with their other job responsibilities. They work under the supervision of *Black Belts* and help achieve the overall results.

The results of Six Sigma continue. A research study by a leading management consulting firm indicated that about 35 percent of U.S. companies have a Six Sigma study in place. For its part, with its adherence to its Six Sigma mantra, Motorola has continued to thrive with profits of $4.6 billion on revenues of $36.8 billion in 2005.

See also: Benchmarking; Best Practice; Core Competencies; Made in Japan; Performance Management/Performance Measurement; Total Quality Management (TQM)

Further Reading

Lean Six Sigma For Supply Chain Management: The 10-Step Solution Process, by James W. Martin, McGraw-Hill (2007).
The Six Sigma Leader : How Top Executives Will Prevail In The 21st Century, by Peter S. Pande; foreword by W. James McNerney, Jr., McGraw-Hill (2007).
"Six Sigma: So Yesterday?; In An Innovation Economy, It's No Longer A Cure-All," by Brian Hindo amd Brian Grow. *BusinessWeek,* New York: Jun 11, 2007, Issue 4038; pg. 11.

Skunkworks

Formally, Skunk Works is a registered trademark of Lockheed Martin. Per a Lockheed Martin press release, initially Skunk Works was the informal name for the group "led by Clarence L. 'Kelly' Johnson that produced many of America's most technologically advanced aircraft. . . . [The] Skunk Works has made an indelible mark on aviation history. The Skunk Works is regarded worldwide as one of the most respected design and development names in aeronautics.

During the heat of World War II, Johnson, Lockheed's famed aircraft designer, forged a team of engineers behind tightly closed doors in makeshift facilities in Burbank, California, and designed and developed the P-80 *Shooting Star*, the Air Force's first truly operational jet fighter, in a mere 143 days. Since then, this organization continues within Lockheed Martin and has given shape to many "firsts" such as the F-104 *Starfighter*, the first Mach 2 aircraft; the U-2 reconnaissance aircraft, which is still the highest flying single engine airplane; and the SR-71 *Blackbird* reconnaissance aircraft, which was the first to fly at speeds in excess of Mach 3. The SR 71, which has been retired, is still the highest flying and fastest jet aircraft ever developed (http://www.lockheedmartin.com/wms/findPage .do?dsp=fec&ci=11787&rsbci=0&fti=0&ti=0&sc=400).

More informally, a skunkworks is a secretive project group engaged in product development or enhancement operating outside the bounds of a company's usual research and development process. Some see these "off-line" operations as providing a source of innovation and rejuvenation for a company, while others perceive them as secretive and subversive.

One of the most recent examples of a successful skunkworks project was outlined in a *Fortune* magazine article ("Razr's Edge," June 8, 2006). It described the development of the innovative phone as

In reality, the RAZR—a play on a code name the geeks themselves dreamed up—was hatched in colorless cubicles in exurban Libertyville, an hour's drive north of Chicago. It was a skunkworks project whose tight-knit team repeatedly flouted Motorola's own rules for developing new products. They kept the project top-secret, even from their colleagues. They used materials and techniques Motorola had never tried before. After contentious internal battles, they threw out accepted models of what a mobile telephone should look and feel like.

In short, the team that created the RAZR broke the mold, and in the process rejuvenated the company.

Other successful skunkwork projects have been the Toshiba laptop and the Xerox Alto. Skunkworks projects are not always viewed positively. For example, an earlier *Fortune* article by Michael Schrage notes, "What's That Bad Odor at Innovation Skunkworks?" (*Fortune*, December 22, 1999). "When an enterprise goes skunk, what's the real message? Top management effectively acknowledges that their corporation is incapable of internal organic innovation and must set up a different organization with different people, different values, and different incentives."

See also: Brainstorming; Competitive Advantage; Empowerment; Intangibles

Further Reading

"M Powered," by Ian Wylie, *Fast Company* magazine, November 2005, page 92, Issue 100.

Skunk Works: A Personal Memoir of My Years of Lockheed, by Ben R. Rich and Leo Janos, Back Bay Books, 1st pbk. ed. (February 1, 1996).

"Skunk Works, 1990s-Style," Peter Gwynne. *Research Technology Management.* Washington: Jul/Aug 1997. Vol. 40, Issue 4; page 18.

Spin-off/Spinout

Most television watchers know what a spin-off is—it is an offshoot of an existing, usually successful television program. In 1974, the popular show *Happy Days* resulted in the spin-off *Laverne and Shirley*. Other more current examples are the spin-off *Frasier* from the popular show *Cheers*, and *CSI Miami* from *CSI*.

While TV shows generally have to be successful to spawn spin-offs, in business the opposite is often the case. From a financial theory point of view, a company as a whole should represent more than the sum of its parts. When that is not the case, managers consider "selling" or spinning off part of their business. In other instances, spin-offs are the result of a government decree when a player is deemed to have an unfair monopoly position in the market. One of the most well-known examples is ATT, the Bell Telephone system, the entity known as Ma Bell. When its break-up was ordered, the company spun into what became known as the Baby Bells (for example Bell South, Verizon).

Fortune magazine ("How to Play the Spin Off Game," March 7, 2005) defined spin-off in two ways. The first was the pure spin-off, where the "parent simply distributes new, publicly traded shares in a division or a subsidiary to its existing shareholders." The other form of spin-off was called a carve-out, where the parent sells only part of the sub or division (typically around 20 percent) to the public through an initial public offering.

In its February 20, 2002, edition, the *Financial Times* offered insight and advice to achieve a successful spin with three key steps. A Booz Allen Hamilton study of all 232 spins by S&P 500 companies in the past decade found that while 26 percent generated extraordinary value, 74 percent underperformed the stock market. The median-performing spin-off generated annual returns for shareholders of 5.7 percentage points in its first two years—worse than the S&P 500.

The first step in a successful spin is ensuring that both parent and spin have viable business and financial structures. On average, companies taking the spin option underperform the S&P 500 by 8 percentage points in the year before the announcement. Spins are often used tactically by management to decorate an unattractive balance sheet. Spun companies are three times more likely than average to fall into bankruptcy because the parent saddles them with excessive debt, onerous contracts, or impaired assets.

The second step in managing a successful spin is to meet or exceed earnings expectations in the first two years, when Wall Street is forming its view of a new management team. Booz Allen's analysis suggests that, in this period, an earnings shortfall has a greater effect on the stock price of a spin-off than on the average publicly traded company.

The third step in a successful spin—and the place where most fall short—is continued growth. Growth is more of a challenge for spins because many are spawned by the desire to separate and sell off a poor-performing or low-growth business.

See also: Lean Manufacturing; Outsourcing; Reengineering; Strategic Alliances

Further Reading

"A Positive Spin on Spinoffs," by Anne Kates Smith, *Kiplinger's Personal Finance*. Washington: Jul 2007. Vol. 61, Issue 7; pp. 14–15.

Spin-Off To Pay-Off : An Analytical Guide To Investing In Corporate Divestitures,
    by Joseph W. Cornell, McGraw-Hill (1998)

Spin-Offs and Equity Carve-Outs, by James A. Miles, J. Randall Woodridge, J.
    Randall Woolridge, and Mark Tocchet, Financial Executives Research Foun-
    dation, 1st ed. (May 1, 1999)

Stakeholder Theory/Management

In 1984, R. Edward Freeman published the book *Strategic Management: A Stakeholder Approach* (Marshfield, MA, Pittman Publishing). The book argued that effective management of the firm went beyond creating shareholder value. The book argued that others, called stakeholders, were also of strategic importance. For Freeman, a stakeholder was more than a shareholder; it "was any group or individual who can affect or who is affected by the achievement of a firm's objectives" (p. 25), and might include customers, employees, suppliers, government, and communities.

The notion that a company would consider the impact on others beyond shareholders was revolutionary, though one that has gained acceptance over time. In "The Lessons from Stakeholder Theory for U.S. Business Leaders (*Business Horizons,* 2005, 48, 255–264), author Ronald Clement of the Kelley School of Business at Indiana offered observations learned from the stakeholder model that were of importance to business. Three of those observations were that:

- Corporations are facing increasing pressures to respond to stakeholders. Pressure is coming from varied sources including the movement to make socially responsible investments, employee attitudes toward work, and customers that want to purchase from socially responsible companies (seen in the success of cause marketing programs).
- Corporations have a legal basis for responding to a broad range of stakeholders. This has been established by legislation that limits pollution and other environmental factors.
- Corporations could improve the bottom line by responding to stakeholder concerns.

One of the more obvious examples of a corporate response to stakeholder concerns has been the recent actions of Wal-Mart. In recent years, the discounter has grown tremendously, from Sam Walton's small store in

Bentonville, Arkansas, to a mega-corporation with sales of $315 billion in its fiscal year 2006. As it continued to grow, it opened larger and larger stores, and according to some with an extreme view Wal-Mart also squeezed out local competition, drove suppliers to the edge of bankruptcy, and took advantage of poorly educated workers by offering low wages and minimal benefits. Backlashes began against Wal-Mart, with "Stop Wal-Mart" campaigns in some areas targeted for development. Faced with such a wave, Wal-Mart took an active hand in addressing these stakeholder groups' communities—about the positive benefits that a Wal-Mart store brings, such as lower prices and opportunities for employment. Importantly Wal-Mart took its campaign to potential employees and customers, with advertising to highlight employee advancement and other qualities that Wal-Mart offered.

Another way to consider stakeholder management is at a personal level. To be effective, one needs to sell ideas, not only to one's immediate boss, but also to subordinates and also peers internally in the organization, and perhaps external audiences as well—key customers, legislators, or even bankers or other capital providers. Several techniques have been suggested, most having two levels. The first is to recognize who the stakeholders are and the second is to prioritize them in some way so as to effectively meet their needs. The World Bank suggests the following attributes to consider in a stakeholder analysis: the stakeholders' position on an issue, the level of influence (power) they hold, the level of interest they have in an issue, and the group with which they are associated (http://www1.worldbank .org/publicsector/anticorrupt/PoliticalEconomy/stakeholderanalysis.htm). Generally speaking, those with high levels of power and high levels of interest should be managed closely; those with high interest but low power would be kept informed; those with high power and low interest would be kept satisfied, while minimal effort would be expended toward those with low power and low interest.

See also: Shareholder Value

Further Reading

The Lessons from Stakeholder Theory for U.S. Business Leaders, by Ronald W. Clement, Greenwich: Business Horizons. May/Jun 2005. Vol. 48, Issue 3; pg. 255.

Redefining the Corporation: Stakeholder Management and Organizational Wealth, by James Post, Lee Preston, and Sybille Sachs, Stanford Business Books, 1st ed. (April 16, 2002).

Stakeholder Theory and Organizational Ethics, by Robert Phillips, 1st ed., San
   Francisco: Berrett-Koehler (2003).

Strategic Alliances

The consulting company Bain and Company defines strategic alliances as
"agreements between firms in which each commits resources to achieve a
common set of objectives" that may include accessing new technology,
improving products or product quality, or entering new markets. "Companies may form strategic alliances with a wide variety of players: customers,
suppliers, competitors, universities, or divisions of government. Through
strategic alliances, companies can improve competitive positioning, gain
entry to new markets, supplement critical skills and share the risk or cost
of major development projects" (http://www.bain.com/management_
tools/tools_alliances.asp?groupCode=2).

Further, Bain recommends that firms seeking a successful strategic alliance take the following steps:

- Define their business vision and strategy in order to understand
  how an alliance fits their objectives;
- Evaluate and select potential partners based on the level of synergy
  and the ability of the firms to work together;
- Develop a working relationship and mutual recognition of opportunities with the prospective partner;
- Negotiate and implement a formal agreement that includes systems
  to monitor performance (http://www.bain.com/management_
  tools/tools_alliances.asp?groupCode=2).

While the pull of a strategic alliance is strong, actual execution of a successful strategic alliance has proven elusive for many. As the authors of
"How to Make Strategic Alliances Work" (*MIT Sloan Management Review*, Summer 2001, p. 37) note:

Strategic alliances—a fast and flexible way to access complementary
resources and skills that reside in other companies—have become an
important tool for achieving sustainable competitive advantage. . . .
Currently the top 500 global companies have an average of sixty ma-

---

Why I Do This: Physician Assistant in Emergency Medicine
Scott Purrone

Physician assistants (PAs) are health care professionals licensed to practice medicine with physician supervision. As part of their comprehensive responsibilities, PAs conduct physical exams, diagnose and treat illnesses, order and interpret tests, counsel on preventive health care, assist in surgery, and in virtually all states can write prescriptions. Within the physician–PA relationship, physician assistants exercise autonomy in medical decision making and provide a broad range of diagnostic and therapeutic services. A PA's practice may also include education, research, and administrative services.

Because of the close working relationship the PAs have with physicians, PAs are educated in the medical model designed to complement physician training. Upon graduation, physician assistants take a national certification examination. To maintain their national certification, PAs must log 100 hours of continuing medical education every two years and sit for a recertification every six years. Graduation from an accredited physician assistant program and passage of the national certifying exam are required for state licensure.

I am a physician assistant who practices in emergency medicine. I usually work about 32–40 hours per week, mostly evening/night shift. A typical shift for me involves me running a minor care area of the emergency department for five and a half hours and then moving up to the main emergency department seeing all levels of ill patients. I perform a majority of the procedures in the ED (sutures, fracture reductions, etc.). I enjoy what I do because in emergency medicine, you never know what is going to walk through the door and how you may help. One minute it could be very slow and the next minute can be very busy. It is also a very challenging occupation because a lot of the time, you are playing medical detective. The nice thing is, you have physician supervision to back you up.

I highly recommend considering this career if you are interested in medicine. The salary is good as is the lifestyle. The other nice benefit is, if you get tired of one specialty, you can always switch to another without going back to school.

---

jor strategic alliances each. Yet alliances are fraught with risks, and almost half fail.

They recommend developing a dedicated division to execute and manage strategic alliances in order to create a higher success rate. The strategic alliance division would be responsible for the "life-cycle" of the alliances: identifying and building the business case, assessing and selecting potential partners, negotiating the agreements between the parties, managing the alliance, assessing its continued contribution to the value of the organization and ultimately overseeing its termination.

Despite the perils, some companies thrive on strategic alliances. For example, *Fortune* magazine says (in "Are Strategic Alliances Working?" September 21, 1992), "Corning, the $3 billion-a-year, glass and ceramics maker is renowned for making partnerships work." The article goes on to cite Corning's relationships with Dow, Siemens (from Germany), and Vitor (from Mexico) and continues that "Alliances are so central to Corning's strategy that the corporation now defines itself as a 'network of organizations.'"

See also: Business-to-Business/Business-to-Consumer (B2B/B2C); Competitive Advantage; Scenario Planning; Value Proposition

Further Reading

Mastering Alliance Strategy: A Comprehensive Guide to Design, Management, and Organization (Jossey Bass Business and Management Series) by James D. Bamford, Benjamin Gomes-Casseres, and Michael S. Robinson, Jossey-Bass (December 27, 2002).

"Politics & Economics: Steelmakers Seek New Tie-Ups That Are Short of True Mergers," Paul Glader, *Wall Street Journal*. New York: Oct 13, 2006. pg. A.4.

Strategic Alliances: An Entrepreneurial Approach to Globalization, by Michael Y. Yoshino, and U. Srinivasa Rangan, Harvard Business School Press (April 1995).

Suggestion Box

A suggestion box is a place for people to offer new ideas and solutions to old problems. Often it is quite literally a box, usually locked so that no one can tamper with its contents.

More recently, the suggestion box has taken an electronic form. Customers are often encouraged to put suggestions into the box to improve products or services. Employee suggestion boxes offer an opportunity for people in the organization to raise concerns about an issue, suggest an improvement to a process, or even report wrongdoing in an organization. Most organizations leave the choice of including his/her name open to the individual submitting something to the suggestion box.

Yet many organizations find their suggestion boxes empty. Some people, especially customers, may not want to invest their time in improving another's company. Others might avoid using a suggestion box because communication is open and they go straight to their supervisor with suggestions. Yet another group fails to use the suggestion box because they fear recrimination and a culture of "shooting the messenger." Even though the box may be anonymous, those in this group are concerned that the suggestion could and would be traced back to them with dire consequences.

Yet, as the *New York Times* noted in "The Silent May Have Something to Say" (November 5, 2006), "Companies lose more than creative ideas when employees feel muzzled. People who feel they cannot or should not speak their mind at work often become less engaged in their work. That in turn means they are less inclined to give their all to their jobs, and increases the odds that they will leave if another opportunity comes along.

"While many employers say they want all kinds of ideas, tips, and criticism from their employees, they have often done little more than hang up a suggestion box—something even the eighth shogun of Japan managed to do outside his palace in the eighteenth century." The article went on to discuss how more companies are trying to improve communications channels with employees using methods such as brainstorming sessions and tools such as company intranets.

See also: Brainstorming; Empowerment; General Electric (GE) Workout; Intellectual Capital; Learning Organization

Further Reading

"Encouraging Suggestive Behavior," by Barry Nalebuff, and Ian Ayres. *Harvard Business Review*. Boston: Dec 2004. Vol. 82, Iss. 12; pg. 18.
"Stuff the Suggestions Box," by Geoffrey C. Lloyd. *Total Quality Management*. Abingdon: Aug 1999. Vol. 10, Issue 6; pg. 869.

Supply Chain

A "supply chain" refers to the entire process of bringing a product to market, beginning with raw materials and ending with the sale of the final product to the customer. This "chain," also known as a logistics network, is comprised of all of the departments, functions, information, and resources involved in producing and supplying the product to the customer.

Most corporations seek to optimize the activities of their supply chain as a way of gaining competitive advantage. This process is known as "supply chain management." The term "supply chain management" was first used by a Booz Allen Hamilton consultant in 1982, as companies realized the value of strategically managing the supply chain processes.

The primary objective of supply chain management is to meet customer demands in as timely a manner as possible, through the most efficient and economical use of resources. These resources include distribution capacity, inventory, and labor.

Supply chain management includes the planning and oversight of all of the processes of the supply chain, including materials, information, and financials, both internally and externally. Additionally, supply chain management includes coordination with channel partners and key suppliers.

Different models have been developed to manage and optimize these activities for efficiency and economy. Two well-known models include SCOR®, a model developed by the Supply-Chain Management Council, and the SCM® model, developed by The Global Supply Chain Forum (GSCF). Each of the processes involves its own set of tracking, key metrics, etc. Supply chain management software assists in managing this effort.

Software facilitates the flow of supply chain information. This, combined with accurate inputs, results in the ability to make or ship only as much of a product as needed. This practice is known as "just-in-time manufacturing." The goal is to reduce the amount of inventory a company keeps on hand. Lower levels of inventory can cut costs dramatically, since there is less production of surplus goods and their accompanying storage costs.

Although different industries have somewhat differing processes, the activities of the supply chain tend to be somewhat similar across organizations and involve the basic steps outlined below.

1. *Planning*: The first step in supply chain management is the development of a plan for managing the resources essential to meeting customer demand for a company's product or service. Another key planning activity is the development and implementation of a set of metrics. These should be designed to monitor and assess each supply chain activity for efficiency, costs, and high quality customer value.

2. *Sourcing*: Second, identify key suppliers to deliver the raw materials, goods, and services required for the end product. Design pric-

ing, payment, and delivery processes. Develop systems for managing inventory of goods received from suppliers.

3. *Manufacturing*: Next, establish a timetable for all elements of product production, including testing, packaging, and readying for delivery. Key metrics at this stage include product quality measurement, production output, and worker productivity.

4. *Delivery*: This is also referred to as the logistical phase. This involves the implementation of processes to receive customer orders, invoice customers, development of a network of warehouses to distribute the product, and select carriers to deliver product.

5. *Returns*: Develop procedures for the return of defective product and offer technical support to customers who are experiencing difficulty.

See also: Just-in-Time; Lean Manufacturing; Mass Customization; Outsourcing; Strategic Alliances

Further Reading

"Keeping the Supply Chain in Focus," by Roger Morton, *Logistics Today*. Cleveland: Jul 2007. Vol. 48, Issue 7; pg. 12.

Supply Chain Management, by Sunil Chopra and Peter Meindl, Prentice Hall, 3rd ed. (March 28, 2006).

Supply Chain Management Best Practices, by David Blanchard, Wiley (December 5, 2006).

Sustainability

Until recently the word sustainability in business was associated with "sustainable" competitive advantage—a lasting advantage that would not be immediately replicable by its competitors. Microsoft is an example of a company with this type of sustainability.

Built to Last by James Collins and Jerry Porras drew on a six-year research project at the Stanford University Graduate School of Business, took eighteen long lasting companies that had outperformed the stock market, and sought to determine the factors that made them exceptional. As *Fast Company* ("Was Built to Last to Last," November, 2004) summarized, "The authors discovered that the visionary companies did certain things very differently from their duller rivals, things that in large part were more about the internal than the external and had little to do with technology or number crunching. Among these were having 'cult-like cultures;' adhering to an ideology that went beyond the simple pursuit of profits; relying on homegrown management; focusing on creating a lasting organization-called 'clock building,' as opposed to 'time telling;' and having the ability to see things not as either-or propositions (the 'genius of the "and,"' in the authors' words, as opposed to the 'tyranny of the "or"')." "A visionary company," they wrote, "doesn't simply balance between preserving a tightly held core ideology and stimulating vigorous change and movement; it does both to the extreme."

With most companies wanting sustainability and to be "built to last," the book became a bestseller, selling over 3.5 million copies worldwide.

More recently sustainability has become associated with a company's contribution to the environment. The EPA (www.epa.gov/sustainability) defines sustainability as "the ability to achieve continuing economic prosperity while protecting the natural systems of the planet and providing a high quality of life for its people. Achieving sustainable solutions calls for stewardship, with everyone taking responsibility for solving the problems of today and tomorrow—individuals, communities, businesses, and governments are all stewards of the environment."

The EPA provides more insight on sustainability with:

Common use of the term "sustainability," in the context of modern environmentalism, began with the publication of the World Commission on Environment and Development report, "Our Common Future," in 1987. Also known as the Brundtland Report, this document characterized sustainable development as "development that meets the needs of the present without compromising the ability of future generations to meet their own needs." This concept of sustainability encompasses ideas, aspirations and values that continue to inspire public and private organizations to become better stewards of the environment and promote positive economic growth and social objectives. The principles of sustainability can stimulate technological innovation, advance competitiveness and improve our quality of life (www.epa.gov/sustainability/basicinfo.htm#what).

As corporations have embraced the environmental notion of sustainability, they have begun to report some progress, at least in terms of how they identify themselves as environmentally responsible. For example, UPS, the delivery service, issued its first Corporate Sustainability Report in 2003 that indicated its vision, strategy, and goals in this area, along with its key performance indicators for marking achievement toward its goals.

Another example is Procter & Gamble. Within its website http://www-.pg.com/company/our_commitment/social_responsibility.jhtml, P&G reports on its social responsibility, highlighting the company's commitment to "caring for our communities, environment, and sustainability." Within sustainability, P&G provides access to a Sustainability Report and notes,

P&G directly contributes to sustainable development by providing products and services that improve the lives of consumers, whether in terms of health, hygiene, or convenience. Through our activities, we also contribute to the economic and social well-being of a range of other stakeholders, including employees, shareholders, local communities in which we operate, and more widely to regional, national, and international development. So, P&G contributes to sustainable development both through "what we do" and "how we do it"

See also: Competitive Advantage; Intangibles; Intellectual Capital; Six Sigma; Value Proposition

Further Reading

The Next Sustainability Wave: Building Boardroom Buy-in (Conscientious Commerce), by Bob Willard and Hunter Lovins, New Society Publishers (April 2005).

The Sustainability Handbook : The Complete Management Guide To Achieving Social, Economic, And Environmental Responsibility, by William R. Blackburn, Environmental Law Institute (2007).

"Working with the Enemy," by Danielle Sacks, and Charles Fishman. *Fast Company.* Boston: Sep 2007, Issue 118; pg. 74.

SWOT Analysis

A SWOT analysis is a strategic planning tool. A SWOT (strengths, weaknesses, opportunities, and threats) Analysis is different from a SWAT (special weapons and tactics) team. The goal of a SWOT analysis is to provide a snap-shot of a company's position at a specific point in time, and from that undertake actions that will improve its competitive position—perhaps even requiring the actions of a corporate-equivalent SWAT team.

The origins of SWOT analysis can be traced to research conducted at the Stanford Research Institute by Robert Stewart and Albert Humphrey during the 1960s. The research was funded by Fortune 500 companies and sought to address the issue of "why corporate planning in terms of long-range planning was not working, did not pay off, and was an expensive investment in futility," and to develop a solution to this problem.

The continued use of the analysis is testament to its usefulness. A thorough SWOT analysis is more than a back-of-the-envelope listing of bullet points; it is a thorough study of each of the elements of the analysis. Additionally, each of the elements needs to be considered in light of a specific goal.

Strengths

What are the company's internal strengths as it seeks to achieve its goal? The answer can be varied. Some potential strengths are proprietary products, strong management, superior quality, or excellent supplier relationships. Strengths should be calibrated absolutely and relative to industry competition. For example, you may believe that product quality is a "strength," but if you score poorly on quality in customer surveys, it may be a weakness instead.

Weaknesses

What are the company's weaknesses as it seeks to achieve its goal? At times weaknesses can be the opposite of strengths. Possible weaknesses could be a lack of talent, poor brands, high manufacturing costs, or strained distribution relationships.

Why I Do This: Museum Interpreter
Ellie Sipkins

When you are a museum interpreter, you have an adventure every working day. Just when you think you have your head full of knowledge to share with the guests, you learn something new.

Usually, the house itself is a treasure of amazing and beautiful architecture and decorative arts. But when you are giving people a tour, and telling stories about the people who lived there, the house suddenly takes on a personality as well. And, as you continue to have the opportunity to share your knowledge, you find that members of the tour often have information to share with you as well.

When you begin a tour, you accompany a group of strangers. But when you reach the last room, you often find that not only are the strangers your friends, but that they have become friends with each other. The warm applause and the comments about how knowledgeable you are, what a great tour it was, and what a wonderful guide you are give you all the joy you could wish for from a job.

If you have a willingness to learn many different things, and you are comfortable being with and talking to groups of people, and you have a desire to have them leave knowing about the house and have a great time doing it, you will be a happy museum interpreter. These are your qualifications.

Finding a museum is not difficult, and most historic houses are in need of willing applicants. The pay, however, is often much less than you'd make at other, more prestigious jobs. You share the available funds with a house that is always hungry for repairs and updates.

If you choose the profession, though, it can be a steppingstone to other exciting careers. For example, you'll have the opportunity to meet craftsman specializing in a variety of areas of expertise, and you'll learn about their jobs. You'll meet decorative arts conservators, architecture conservators, people who reproduce antique painted surfaces, people who repair old clocks, reproduce colored class, and help to preserve every conceivable thing. You might see a nineteenth-century painting being faithfully reproduced by twenty-first century techniques. You'll learn about all of the different kinds of jobs that weave in and around what you are doing.

Being a museum interpreter in an historic house is the gateway to a fascinating world where the past is meeting the future every time you say, "Hello, Welcome to our house!"

Opportunities

While strengths and weaknesses are internal to the firm, opportunities and threats are those factors found external to the firm. Opportunities might be emerging technology (such was the case with expansion of the Internet in the 1990s), reduction in regulation (deregulation of telecommunications or the airline industry sparked new opportunities), or a new customer need.

Threats

Threats include any opponent to a company's well-being. They are often related to actions taken by a competitor: a new competitor, a competitor's new and innovative product or service, a price war, etc. A threat could also come from an action taken by a third party, such as a new tax or environmental legislation that affects your company. Finally, a threat can come from other causes, such as a change in weather patterns or a downward trend in the economy.

By 2004, SWOT analysis had been "fully developed, and proven to cope with today's problems of setting and agreeing realistic annual objectives without depending on outside consultants or expensive staff resources," according to Humphrey (see http://www.businessballs.com/swotanalysis freetemplate.htm). It is still a popular analysis tool today.

See also: Benchmarking; Mission Statement; Scenario Planning

Further Reading

"Performing a SWOT analysis. (Checklist 005) (strengths weaknesses opportunities threats)," *Chartered Management Institute: Checklists: Marketing Strategy,* by Thomson Gale, October 1, 2005.

Strategic Management and Business Analysis, by David Williamson, Peter Cooke, Wyn Jenkins, and Keith Michael Moreton, Butterworth-Heinemann, pap/cdr. ed. (December 17, 2003).

"Using a Market Analysis," by Jack Brennan, *Golf Course News,* Yarmouth: Feb 2005. Vol. 17, Issue 2; pg. 22.

Synergy

Can one plus one ever be more than two? In the world of business mergers, firms are always looking for such a Holy Grail: a new, combined company greater than the sum of its parts. Synergy is just that, and companies search harder for it than Arthur's knights did the Grail. Unfortunately, false grails abound, and while the search for synergy is exhaustive, actually finding it and enjoying it is elusive.

Thus, synergy is often cited as the driving force behind a merger or acquisition, as seen in the AOL–Time Warner merger. *BusinessWeek* noted in an article titled "AOL has No Future," January 27, 2003, "that AOL Time Warner has been talking about synergy and multimedia millions for three years now. But the payoff keeps getting pushed back, and the burden of AOL grows heavier by the day. Now, as Stephen M. Case prepares to step down as chairman of the combined company, directors should snap to their senses and dump the Internet unit. Sell it. Spin it off. Give it away, if need be. The magic is gone."

Again the power of synergy was a driver of Procter and Gamble's acquisition of Gillette. *Time* magazine quoted P&G's CEO in a February 7, 2005, article titled "Land of the Giants P&G's Megadeal with Gillette is Just the Latest in a New Wave of Merger Mania. Investors Beware," "The hardest advantage to measure is that merger buzzword synergy. P&G knows a lot about women. Gillette knows a lot about men," Lafley [P&G's CEO] told investors. "It's very simple, but it's a potent combination."

In the same article, Robert McDonald, a P&G senior executive, hinted to *Time* that new products that could capitalize on each firm's strengths. "We have the best-selling male fragrance in Hugo Boss," he says, "How about a Hugo Boss designer razor?"

Synergy is difficult to achieve. Yet it is a constant attraction for companies looking to spark marketplace winners. For example, when CVS (the retail drug store) acquired Caremark, a pharmacy benefit manager, in 2006, the *Wall Street Journal* noted ("CVS, Caremark Unite to Create Drug-Sale Giant," November 2, 2006)

> The combined company could realize strategic benefits over both its archrivals. CVS and Caremark said they would gain $400 million in "operating synergies"—increased purchasing power and cost savings—via the deal. CVS could also use its retailing leverage to run promotions on items like beauty aids at its 6,200 outlets to attract

new PBM clients. Conversely, Caremark has tens of millions of members, translating into a potential windfall of new foot traffic to CVS stores.

The results of this acquisition have yet to be seen.

See also: Spin-off/Spinout; Strategic Alliances

Further Reading

Alignment: Using the Balanced Scorecard to Create Corporate Synergies, by Robert S. Kaplan and David P. Norton, Harvard Business School Press (April 24, 2006).

"Coevolving: At last, A Way to Make Synergies Work," by Kathleen M. Eisenhardt, and D. Charles Galunic, *Harvard Business Review*, Boston: Jan/Feb 2000. Vol. 78, Issue 1; p. 91.

The Synergy Trap, by Mark L. Sirower, Free Press (January 23, 1997).

T

Telework

The term telework refers to the use of telecommunications to substitute for physical business travel. Telework typically includes use of a variety of telecommunications, tools such as the phone, fax, e-mail, video conferencing, webconnections and others for travel either to an office or distant meeting. Physicist and engineer Jack Nilles coined the terms "telecommuting" and "telework" in 1973 when he was a professor at the University of Southern California (USC) and Director for Interdisciplinary Research there.

Nilles went on to found the consulting firm, JALA International in 1980. According to the JALA website (www.jala.com), Nilles is known as the "father of telecommuting/teleworking," and he has "developed and/or evaluated telecommuting projects for a variety of Fortune 100 companies, the state governments of California, Arizona, and Washington, the city of Los Angeles, and other companies and organizations in the United States, Europe, and South America.

Sales representatives who travel from one customer to another throughout the day or week were the early pioneers of this type of work. Business consultants have also made use of telework options for decades when they spend large portions of their workday or work week at a client's business rather than at their employers' office.

Now, telework is often widely practiced across many different functions within many types of businesses. Telework may include employees who work from home or a satellite office or from their car in place of the traditional desk job at the company's physical building. Telework also includes situations in which employees from multiple offices, working together as a team, schedule videoconferencing meetings or conference calls that replace expensive and time-consuming travel to a single meeting place. In addition, many self-employed professionals "telework" from home offices.

The expanding field of distance learning is also a type of telework where the teachers and students do not need to be in the same classroom to conduct class but have access to shared electronic space that is used to

---

Why I Do This: Business Analyst, Financial Services Industry
Michael Goodwin

The primary responsibility of my job is gathering detailed business require-ments to build or enhance on-line information delivery platforms (web ap-plications) and provide support for them. I work with the application users (clients and internal staff) to define the requirements and ensure the devel-opment staff understands what is being requested. When the finished prod-uct is complete I coordinate the set up of access to the web application and provide training on its functions and features. I provide product sup-port to the users when they encounter a problem or require assistance re-trieving a desired set of results or if they have questions about the results they received. I resolve the problems when possible and the problems which cannot be resolved immediately are documented in detail for review and resolution by the development team. I also coordinate meetings to ob-tain updates from the development staff and provide updates to the clients.

I graduated from college with a BS in Business Administration as an ac-counting major. I was offered a job through a friend of a friend at a finan-cial services company. The thing I like most about my job is the interac-tion with people and the satisfaction I get from helping people who are experiencing problems using the application. I initially went into this line of work because of the job stability in the financial services industry and the financial compensation. A person with personality traits and skills that I feel would enjoy this job are attention to detail, ability to communicate ver-bally and in writing, people oriented, and the ability to problem solve.

At the present time, I have chosen to pursue a career change now be-cause I am not happy with my chosen profession. And so the message I have for people trying to decide on their career is: Do not to base your de-cision on financial compensation alone—rather, consider what you like to do and where you want to live.

---

exchange information between the teacher and students or among stu-dents.

The benefits of telework can be great and varied. These include reduced commuting costs and time, increased productivity, more flexible "office hours," and greater job satisfaction. Some teleworkers find that with re-duced commute time, they have more time for leisure activities or family time, which creates less stress from work and less resentment of work's im-position on other pursuits. On a broader level, telework can reduce overall congestion on the roads, decrease the use of gasoline, and cause less of an impact on the environment than more traditional working arrangements.

For employers, providing a telework option can also increase retention rates among employees who are trying to balance work and family demands. Telework can be used as a valuable recruiting tool. The costs associated with telework, such as a home based computer and connectivity to the employer's systems, or increase in management time to supervise teleworking staff, can generally be offset by the overall benefits of telework arrangements.

Employers who consider implementing telework options in response to employee requests or a part of their own business model for reducing overhead costs, often find that there are some job categories and some types of jobs that lend themselves to telework better than others. Writers and editors, for example, can generally work from remote locations quite easily. Additionally, some employers find that it is possible to offer the option of telework for one or two days per week but that employees need to spend a significant portion of their work week in more traditional offices. It is also critical for any manager or employer considering telework arrangements to clarify the performance criteria and expectations so that both teleworks and non-teleworks are clear on what is expected of the teleworkers when they are not in the office.

Yet telework is not for everyone. Some employees working outside the office, find themselves isolated with the lack of co-workers and frustrated by what it means to run an office off-site (dealing with telecommunications and technology glitches). Even for the most tech-savvy, there is a certain amount of ramping up time. It can be difficult to get used to a work-world where, in a traditional office setting, an employee might "brainstorm" with a colleague in a spur-of-the-moment meeting. In a telework situation, most if not all "meetings" must be scheduled.

In the past few years, "telework" has become, to many, just plain work, according to a study conducted by the Telework Coalition in 2006. According to the Telework Coalition press release, the study (which was sponsored by Intel) examined private and public sector employers representing more than 500,000 employees and almost 150,000 teleworkers and "mobile" workers. The press release said that the study "looked at how these large organizations addressed and overcame obstacles and objections to create successful programs that benefit both the organization and its employees through reduced real estate costs, increased employee retention, and a much higher rate of employee satisfaction."

According to Chuck Wilsker, president and CEO of the Telework Coalition, who was quoted in the press release: "An important finding is that virtual work, mobile work, telecommuting, telework, or distributed work, whatever it is called, is now regarded as 'Just Work.' Most study participants emphasized the importance of the mobility that telework enables when dealing in a global economy. Whenever, and wherever the job can best be done, it gets done."

"As long as employees have a laptop, high speed Internet access, and a phone, they are in business wherever they are. And, with the convergence of these three technologies, whether a wireless equipped laptop with a VoIP phone, or a new generation PDA, work can be done from almost anywhere," he said (www.telcoa.org, press release entitled "Benchmarking Study Finds 'Telework' has Evolved into a Mainstream Way of Working; Now, 'It's Just Work'" dated March 9, 2006).

See also: Flex-Time; War for Talent

Further Reading

Association for Commuter Transportation (www.actweb.org) is a non-profit organization supporting TDM programs.

ecommute (www.ecommute.net/program) is a U.S. federal government sponsored study of the impacts and benefits of telecommuting.

Home Computing Initiatives (www.dti.gov.uk/hci) is a website that describes how employers can implement Home Computing Initiatives.

Smarter Choices—Changing the Way We Travel, by Sally Cairns, et al., UK Department for Transport (www.dft.gov.uk), July 2004. This comprehensive study provides detailed evaluation of the potential travel impacts and costs of various mobility management strategies.

Teletrips (www.teletrips.com) promotes the benefits of Telework and other TDM strategies.

Virtual Mobility Website (www.virtual-mobility.com) is an information site sponsored by the UK Department for Transport, Local Government and the Regions.

http://eto.org.uk (European Telework Online)

www.ivc.ca (Canadian Telework Association)

www.telecommute.org (International Telework Association)

Signs of Changing Culture:
Telecommuting Today: A Snapshot

"Work at Home Summary" by the Bureau of Labor Statistics of the U.S. Department of Labor. September 22, 2005. http://www.bls.gov/news .release/homey.nr0.htm

The likelihood of working at home varies greatly by occupation. This is not surprising, since some jobs are more readily done away from the workplace than others. Almost 30 percent of workers in management, professional, and related occupations reported working at home in May 2004. Nearly two-thirds of persons who usually worked at home were employed in these occupations.

About one in five sales workers usually worked at home. In contrast, only 3 percent of workers in production, transportation, and material moving occupations performed job-related work at home. From an industry perspective, workers employed in professional and business services, in financial activities, and in education and health services were among those most likely to work at home in 2004.

Temporary Workers

In the workforce there are full- and part-time workers and another category called temporary workers. Temporary workers, or "temps," work for a period of time in a job to fill a void in the regular workforce. That void might be caused by a surge in demand, a maternity leave, or an illness.

The Department of Labor defines temporary workers as those in "contingent and alternative employment" arrangements. A contingent worker is one who is working without an implicit or explicit contract for ongoing employment. According to the Department of Labor (www.bls.gov/news .release/conemp.nr0.htm), in February 2005 there were about 5.7 million contingent workers in the United States (under its broadest definition) representing about 4 percent of total employment. Another 7.4 percent of the workforce (about 10.3 million workers) were defined as independent contractors (consultants or freelance workers), 1.8 percent were on-call workers, .9 percent were temporary help where a temporary help agency paid them, and another .6 percent were workers provided by contract firms.

Traditionally, "temporary workers" filled unskilled, manual labor jobs. However, "The Changing Temporary Workforce" (*Occupational Outlook Quarterly*, 1999, p. 25) notes that "the image of temporary workers doing repetitive, low-skilled tasks has grown as outdated as the black and white television. Higher skilled workers, ranging from laboratory technicians to lawyers increasingly make themselves available to temporary assignments."

Independent contractors tend to be older than workers in a more traditional arrangement, with 81 percent aged thirty-five or older compared to 65 percent of the "regular" workforce. Also according to the Department of Labor findings these workers were more likely to be in "management, business, and financial operations; sales and related occupations; and construction and extraction occupations." Notably unlike most other temporary workers, independent contracts were in their role by choice, with "fewer than one in ten independent contractors saying they would prefer a more traditional work arrangement."

The rationale for the supply and the demand for temporary workers varies. Some suggest that companies actually are avoiding paying for full time employees with the cost of benefits when they hire temporary workers. Others suggest that the supply of temporary workers has risen with the rise of women in business where educated, well-paid women might prefer temporary assignments to have more flexibility for family life.

Workers in all forms of temporary work arrangements had significantly less access to health insurance and other benefits such as pension plans.

Homeland Security and Temporary Workers

There is another kind of "temporary worker" as defined by the Department of Homeland Security. These are individuals with nonimmigrant visas eligible to work in the United States for a short, defined period of time. According to the State Department website, "The Immigration and Nationality Act provides several categories of nonimmigrant visas for a person who wishes to work temporarily in the United States. There are annual numerical limits on some classifications which are shown in parentheses.

H-1B classification applies to persons in a specialty occupation which requires the theoretical and practical application of a body of highly specialized knowledge requiring completion of a specific course of higher education. This classification requires a labor attestation issued by the Secretary of Labor (65,000). This classification also applies to Government-to-Government research and development, or co-production projects administered by the Department of Defense (100);

H-2A classification applies to temporary or seasonal agricultural workers;

H-2B classification applies to temporary or seasonal nonagricultural workers. This classification requires a temporary labor certification issued by the Secretary of Labor (66,000);

H-3 classification applies to trainees other than medical or academic. This classification also applies to practical training in the education of handicapped children (50) (www.state.gov).

In recent years, there has been increased focus on these temporary workers, as it is believed that many remain in the United States after their temporary work visa has expired. In his 2007 State of the Union address, President George Bush called for the creation of a temporary worker program aimed at this group. Specifically, he noted,

[s]uch a program will serve the needs of our economy by providing a lawful and fair way to match willing employers with willing foreign workers to fill jobs that Americans have not taken. The program will also serve our law enforcement and national security objectives by taking pressure off the border and freeing our hard-working Border Patrol to focus on terrorists, human traffickers, violent criminals, drug runners, and gangs.

The Temporary Worker Program Should Be Grounded
In The Following Principles:

- American Workers Must Be Given Priority Over Guest Workers. Employers should be allowed to hire guest workers only for jobs that Americans have not taken.
- The Program Must Be Truly Temporary. Participation should be for a limited period of time, and the guest workers must return home after their authorized period of stay. Those who fail to return home in accordance with the law should become permanently ineligible for a green card and for citizenship.

- Participation Should Fluctuate With Market Conditions. When the economy is booming, and there are not enough American workers available to help businesses grow, the program should be open to more participants. But when times are tough and Americans struggle to find jobs, the economy cannot and should not support as many guest workers.

See also: Free Agent; Job Sharing

Further Reading

Foreign Temporary Workers in America: Policies that Benefit the U.S. Economy, by Lindsay B. Lowell (ed.), Quorum Books (April 30, 1999).
"Temp Workers Fill Labor Pool" (human resources management), by L. J. Butterfield, *Fairfield County Business Journal* (January 23, 2006), Volume: 45 Issue: 4 Page: 21(1).

Theory X and Theory Y

In his 1960 book *The Human Side of Enterprise*, the American social psychologist Douglas McGregor proposed his now famous XY Theory model of management. Based on research he conducted in organizations during the prior three decades, McGregor argued that managers fundamentally fall into either Theory X or Theory Y styles of management. Theory X and Theory Y are still often referenced in the field of management and motivation, though more recent management experts and studies have questioned the inflexibility of McGregor's model. XY Theory, while not often referred to as such, is still considered a pertinent description of the management of people in organizations.

Theory X, which is characterized as "authoritarian management style," assumes that the average person dislikes work and will do what he or she can to avoid work. Under this assumption, people must be forced to work towards the goals of the organization or risk punishment. Theory X also assumes that people prefer to be directed in their work, to avoid responsibility, are generally lacking in ambition, and want security above all else. Those who employ a Theory X management style consider that their job is to achieve results for the organization despite the people who are responsible for the tasks.

Theory Y, which is characterized as "participative management style," assumes that the average person will put as much effort into work as he or she puts into leisure activities. Under this assumption, people are capable of applying self-control and self-direction to their work to achieve the objectives of the organization without the need for coercion, external control, or threat of punishment. Commitment to and achievement of work objectives is considered to be a result of the rewards and not the threat of punishment associated with their achievements. People not only accept but actively seek out greater responsibility. People with this style of management use greater imagination and creativity in their approach to solving problems and managing the people who work with or for them.

In his work McGregor argues that those managers who tend towards a Theory X style of management generally achieve poor results. On the other hand, McGregor argues that more enlightened managers who tend towards a Theory Y style of management generally produce better performance and results. In addition, Theory Y managers generally allow people whom they manage to grow and develop to a much greater degree than those who use a Theory X style of management.

Despite widely held beliefs that Theory Y management styles are superior to Theory X management styles, Theory X styles still exist and even prevail in many organizations. Working for a Theory X boss can be difficult. These types of managers are known to be results- and deadline-driven, often to the exclusion of everything else. They can be intolerant, aloof, or even arrogant. In extreme situations, they are the managers who have the shortest tempers, demand compliance, and issue threats and edicts. It is not considered common to see a Theory X manager make use of project teams, delegate work, demonstrate concern about staff or morale, or thank or praise others for their efforts or contributions. Worse yet, these managers have been known to apportion blame rather than learn from experience. They do not welcome suggestions from others with different perspectives. Managers with this management style will be resistant to feedback, particularly from peers or subordinates, and unable to hear feedback as anything more than criticism from superiors. In general, these managers are unhappy individuals, particularly at work but often in their personal lives as well.

There are a variety of approaches that may help individuals to successfully manage their Theory X bosses. Perhaps the best advice is to avoid confrontation with a Theory X manager and focus on achieving results, on time, and on budget. Since Theory X managers are very concerned with facts and figures, work for these individuals should be measurable and reportable. Refrain from including information that might be considered inconsequential such as the human factors or soft issues. And deliver on your commitments or risk retribution. If you consistently deliver results to a Theory X manager, you will earn the right to approach your tasks with less oversight in the future. This approach is considered to be the only approach that will be successful when managing upwards with Theory X bosses.

While McGregor's Theory X and Theory Y management and motivation model revolutionized much of management theory, there are critics of his model. Some critics of the model point out that workers today face different work environments than when McGregor conducted his research and that since those workers and managers have much greater job insecurity, the workplace and culture of enterprises today reinforces Theory X styles of management. Other critics argue that McGregor's model assumes that any manager or individual is capable of changing management styles when confronted with the apparent superiority of one style over another. McGregor's critics claim that the apparent failure of Theory X management styles is merely a mismatch of management style with personality style and that by better matching management styles to individuals, either style could and would be effective. These critics argue that this is precisely why Theory X management styles still exist and in fact in some organizations are quite common. If this is true, then effective training for managers becomes more complex and might involve a greater understanding of how to fit the managers, the teams, team members, and tasks to take greater advantage of the diverse set of abilities of the individuals involved as well as the business objectives.

See also: Management by Objectives; Open Book Management; Performance Management/Performance Measurement; Stakeholder Theory/Management

Further Reading

"Douglas McGregor: Theory X and Theory Y," *Thinkers* (December 1, 1999).
The Human Side of Enterprise, Annotated Edition, by Douglas McGregor, McGraw-Hill, 1st ed. (December 21, 2005).

360-Degree Feedback

Historically, and traditionally, bosses "reviewed" their employees once a year. And in doing so, many didn't reach much further than their own notebooks for information on which to base their reviews. Today, many more companies are conducting reviews that are the product of much more intensive and complex processes. It's the norm in an increasing numbers of companies, for bosses to ask a person's colleagues, direct reports, and sometimes even customers for their thoughts on how that person is doing, in what areas they excel, and how they might improve their performance going forward.

These newer more inclusive and intensive review processes are commonplace in many professional services firms, but they're also an increasingly "typical" practice in companies across a spectrum of industries.

The idea of "360-feedback" is one way to approach such a review. Simply put, 360-degree feedback means finding out what your boss, your colleagues, your direct reports, and maybe even your customers, think of your performance at work. This type of feedback is also often referred to as "multi-source" feedback. The 360-degree method means that the input comes from above, below, alongside, and sometimes outside. (Sometimes, companies will conduct interviews with important clients to get this sort of feedback; at the other end of the spectrum, a simple e-mail questionnaire asking customers to rate their customer service experience can also provide insights.)

The idea is that it is useful to be aware of how your performance looks from many different perspectives, because what looks good to one party might not look as good to another. If you're a manager, the theory goes, it is just as important to know what your "manag-ees" think of your skill and style as what your own supervisor thinks.

How does the 360-approach help a company? In some cases, it can help leaders better understand how their management style is received in different venues throughout a company. With this understanding, leaders can then calibrate their style to try to be more effective managers to a range of employees.

As noted earlier, there are many methods for conducting high-quality 360-degree feedback. Some companies employ third–party consultants to keep the process objective. Others have formal "input" cycles where employees write short "reviews" of the people they work with and then a manager gathers the reviews and builds a "consensus" review from the pieces. Some top managers hire coaches to conduct these reviews on their behalf, in an attempt to get honest feedback from direct reports who might otherwise be reluctant to speak their minds.

The idea can be intimidating. But consider what Kris Frieswick wrote in *CFO Magazine*, June 1, 2001, in an article entitled "Truth and Consequences: Why Tough '360' Reviews and Employee Ranking are Gaining Fans":

"Working as a senior finance executive at Boeing would be a pretty great job, right?

Before you answer, consider what would happen during your annual review: CFO Michael Sears would gather all your direct reports in a room, where they would discuss your strengths and weaknesses. Then he would confront you with their opinions, citing examples to back him up.

Few finance executives—or anybody for that matter—would be completely comfortable with such a review process. But Sears swears by it. As far as he knows, it hasn't scared anybody off," he says.

Frieswick goes on to write that Sears has used this approach for more than ten years. And that although Sears' techniques is a "particularly intense" variation on the 360-degree approach, that in general, the 360 methods, while controversial, can be a real boon to companies. The issue, Frieswick writes, is that more traditional review methods focus on measuring what employees do, whereas this approach gets at how the work gets done, and what kind of effect it has on colleagues and employees and their abilities or motivation to be productive. (Picture a manager saying, "You got 6,000 reports done in the last year, and you were never late." Could that same manager also be saying, "You scared away three assistants in one year, and the people you gather data from think that your twenty-four-hour turnaround deadlines are unreasonable, and are affecting their productivity. Here's how . . . " Quite possibly. And that's the difference that a 360-degree review can potentially bring to the table, and what a more traditional approach might surface.

Many companies find the technique very useful. But like any tool, it is only as good as the way it is used. 360-degree feedback has a potential downside as well. If the reviews are not conducted objectively, with clear performance goals in mind, strong guidelines for those offering the feedback, and careful management of the results, this type of feedback can quickly become a "gripe-fest" or worse, offering no discernable value to the employee in question, or the company at large.

As Susan Healthfield says, in an article called "360-Degree Feedback: The Good, the Bad, and the Ugly" (www.humanresources.about.com): "As with any performance feedback process, it can provide you with a profoundly supportive, organization-affirming method for promoting employee growth and development. Or, in the worst cases, it saps morale, destroys motivation, enables disenfranchised employees to go for the jugular, or plot and scheme revenge scenarios."

Further Reading

The Art and Science of 360 Degree Feedback," by Richard Lepsinger and Antoinette D. Lucia, Pfeiffer (May 9, 1997).

Maximizing the Value of 360-degree Feedback: A Process for Successful Individual and Organizational Development (J-B CCL [Center for Creative Leadership]) by Walter W. Tornow and Manuel London, Jossey-Bass, 1st ed. (March 23, 1998).

Time Management

Although business has progressed from an eight-hour day to a 24/7 environment, there never seems to be enough time in the day, the week, the month, or even the year for most people to get their jobs done. The work day keeps expanding, but for most there just doesn't seem to be enough time to get it all done. As a result, effective time management skills have become increasingly important. As the Japanese saying goes, "the busier you are, the more on time you have to be," a notion that is opposite to most American norms, where you are permitted to run late when you are busy.

Time management has been an important part of companies' outlooks for nearly the entire history of companies. It is now of paramount importance, as ever-increasing competition leads businesses to use every advantage—and every minute—in order to get ahead (or even just to survive).

Technology has facilitated this desire: PDAs, cell phones, e-mail, and computers in general have revised companies' expectations of their em-

---

Why I Do This: Dental Office Manager
Tracie K. Crowley

I graduated from college in 1978 with a degree in Elementary Education. Teaching jobs were few and far between. I was lucky enough to teach 3rd grade for a year, but then Massachusetts passed Proposition 2½. I had a choice at this point to either substitute and hope for a job or to look for something I could depend upon. I decide to move along.

Several years passed and I had a growing family. It was my choice to put my "career" decisions on the backburner, so I took a couple of "jobs." I was hired by my dentist to fill in as a receptionist. Four years later the dentist decided he wanted to computerize the bookkeeping. I spent many hours enjoying learning and using the dental software. I found it easy to learn and when the owner of the company offered me a job, I accepted.

I spent the next nine years teaching, supporting, and selling computers and dental software to dentists in New England, PA, GA, FL, and Texas. Once a dental office was up and running I would work with the doctor and staff teaching them how to use the system to get the most out of their practice.

Nine years was a long time. I worked directly with about 200 dentists and their office managers. It was exhausting. Now I work for just one dentist. He was a friend of mine many years before he offered me the job. Over the past six years we hired a staff that has become a family and we've worked together to build a very successful dental practice. Daily, I do the scheduling. The schedule is set in terms of production. The doctor's schedule is set so that the procedures he will be doing net the maximum production. Hygiene schedules need to be full with a list of patients to draw upon in case of a cancellation. I process all insurance claims, hygiene recall, banking, payroll, billing, and payments.

My favorite part of the job is our patients. I've known many of them for years. We care about them and they care about us. There is a lot of hand holding in a dental office. Patients are very nervous. I am the first person they meet and it's up to me to put them at ease. Once the doctor and the hygienist have done their part I explain to the patient how to use their insurance and other financing options to pay for the treatments they need.

---

ployees' productivity and spurred still more efforts to harness technology to squeeze even more out of personnel.

There are many sources that offer tools for effective time management. For example, the American Management Association website offers suggestions from Brian Tracy, author of the book *Time Power*. They involve understanding what needs to be done, assigning an importance factor to the items, and adhering to a means to monitor progress. For example:

- Always work from a list. Write down every single task that you want to accomplish in the day.
- Organize your daily list by priority. Organize tasks on a daily basis by understanding its necessity. Categories include must dos down to nice but not essential tasks
- Commit to using any time management system you like. It could be a hand-based system or a spiffy PDA or Blackberry, but what is important is using it regularly until it becomes a habit.

Stephen Covey, author of the book *The Seven Habits of Highly Effective People*, offers the following two-by-two matrix that sorts out the urgent (fire fighting type tasks) and the important tasks that face business people and people in general.

	Urgent	Not Urgent
Important	Quadrant 1	Quadrant 2
Not Important	Quadrant 3	Quadrant 4

Many find themselves operating in Quadrant 1 or Quadrant 3, as the urgent items often override the tasks that can be left for another day (until that day comes). Some find the quadrants helpful in sorting out their to-do lists. Covey advocates spending time in Quadrant 2, as tasks accomplished in this sector are likely to have the more long term benefit for the company. Quadrant 2 activities include tasks like relationship building, planning, prevention, recognizing new opportunities, and recreation.

Yet for all the advice available companies and individuals struggle with time management. In 2003, Marakon Associates and The Economist Intelligence Unit conducted a survey of 187 companies with market values of at least $1 billion to learn how companies invested their time. The results were published in an article in the *Harvard Business Review* (September 2004, "Stop Wasting Valuable Time") and found that senior management spent relatively little time together (averaging twenty-one hours per month), had unfocused and undisciplined ways of setting agendas, and spent too little time on strategic (important) decisions.

The article advocated several techniques to "get time back." Among them:

1. Separate operational decisions from strategic decisions and deal with them separately.
2. Spend time together making decisions rather than having discussion sessions.
3. Assess the value of each agenda item.
4. Remove issues from the agenda expeditiously.
5. Present viable options so that real choices are on the table and decisions can be made.

See also: E-mail; Flex-Time; Intranet/Extranet; Job Sharing; Just-in-Time; 24/7

Further Reading

The Time Trap: The Classic Book on Time Management," by Alec MacKenzie, MJF Books, 3rd ed. (March 2002).

Signs of Changing Culture: A Typical Work Week

"American Time Use Survey Summary" by the Bureau of Labor Statistics (BLS) of the U.S. Department of Labor, July 27, 2006. http://www.bls.gov/news.release/atus.nr0.htm

The Bureau of Labor Statistics (BLS) of the U.S. Department of Labor reported that in 2005:

- Many more people worked on weekdays than on weekend days. About 83 percent of employed persons worked on an average weekday, compared with 32 percent on an average weekend day.
- Employed persons worked 7.5 hours, on average, on the days that they worked. They also worked more hours on weekdays than on weekend days—7.9 versus 5.5 hours.
- Multiple jobholders were about twice as likely to work on a weekend day or holiday as single jobholders.
- On the days they worked, employed men worked about three-quarters of an hour more than employed women. The difference partly reflects women's greater likelihood of working part time.

However, even among full-time workers (those usually working thirty-five hours or more per week) men worked slightly longer than women—8.3 versus 7.7 hours.

- About 74 percent of persons employed in management, business, and financial operations occupations reported working on a given day—a greater share than those employed in any other occupation. Ninety-one percent of people in these occupations worked on a given weekday, as compared to 83 percent of all workers.
- Employed women living with a child under age six spent about an hour less per day working than employed women living in households with no children. On the other hand, employed men living with a child under age six worked about the same amount of time as those living in households with no children.

Total Quality Management (TQM)

In the early 1980s, Hewlett Packard became critical of the quality of U.S.-made computer chips; it had an eye on the Japanese chip makers and other companies, who were developing what would later be known in business parlance as Total Quality Management (TQM). Basically, by checking quality throughout the manufacturing process, a company could create a high quality product that had a better chance of being a hit with consumers, reaping profits and prestige.

Interestingly, while the Japanese brought TQM into vogue, it was an American, W. Edwards Deming, who developed the core principles of TQM. TQM is a customer-focused tool, with quality for the product determined by the customer's needs rather than solely engineering standard. The goal is to satisfy customer needs with quality in the most economical way. TQM is also employee focused, allowing employees to measure quality, solve problems, and take remedial actions as necessary to deliver the product at the standards demanded by customers.

American companies adopted the principles of TQM after the Japanese proved that quality could be an element of a successful strategy that increased customer satisfaction and reduced costs (less re-working, doing things right the first time, etc.). Companies such as "Hewlett-Packard and

Ford Motor Company in the USA and Canada; British Telecom in the UK; Fujitsu and Toyota in Japan; Crysel in Mexico; and Samsung in South Korea have found success with their respective TQM programs" (Talha Mohhamad, "Total Quality Management (TQM): An Overview," *The Bottom Line*, 2004, Vol. 17, Issue 1, p. 15).

As Mohhamad further notes in his article, "Managers and experts disagree about how to most effectively apply TQM in their organizations. Some advise that customer satisfaction is the driving force behind quality improvement; others suggest quality management is achieved by internal productivity or cost improvement programs; and still others consider TQM as a means to introduce participatory management. In general, the Japanese concentrate on customer satisfaction with a particular focus on understanding customer needs and expectations. Until very recently, Americans in general have emphasized the 'cost of non-conference' and the importance of employees meeting the agreed upon requirements for each process."

TQM was at its most popular in the mid-1990s, but its star has waned as other quality management tools have come along, notably Six Sigma.

See also: Six Sigma

Further Reading

Total Quality Management: Strategies and Techniques Proven at Today's Most Successful Companies, by Stephen George and Arnold Weimerskirch, Wiley, 2nd ed. (February 1998).

Training and Development

One way to think about training and development is that training is learning about doing today's job and development is about gaining the skills to do your next job. Regardless of experience level, almost every employee needs some level of training when entering a new job. It may be limited in scope—perhaps a few hours to learn the ropes of doing the job—or it may be longer term; many days of training if someone is learning a new computer program or needs to master a series of steps in building a product or serving a customer.

Development is more focused on the future, building the skills and experiences that allow employees to grow and advance in the organization.

There are several tools for employee development, including temporary assignments, formal education and training, career development workshops, and coaching and counseling. Recently, the onus for training and development has shifted from "something the company does for the employee" to one where employees are encouraged to be self-learners.

Training and development is acknowledged as a key component to a successful company. If its people are knowledgeable, the firm will be able to adapt to changes in the marketplace and continue to succeed. As *HR* magazine said in "Talent Management in a Knowledge-Based Economy" (May 1, 2006), "In today's knowledge-driven business environment, the importance of ongoing training and development cannot be overstated. Increased global competition and the realities of a global market mean that the skills bar is constantly being raised. Now that organizations (and nations) are competing on the basis of the knowledge and skills of their workforces, employee development takes on a heightened significance. Effective management of workers requires the creation of ongoing opportunities for learning."

See also: Empowerment; Learning Organization; Performance Management/Performance Measurement

Further Reading

Creating, Implementing, & Managing Effective Training & Development: State-of-the-Art Lessons for Practice, by Kurt Kraiger (ed.), Pfeiffer, 1st ed. (November 15, 2001).

Turnaround

A turnaround is exactly what its name implies: turning a business around, usually from losing money to making money. At times, though, a turnaround might entail another kind of change—in attitude, in customer perception, or in innovation.

An effective corporate turnaround requires strong analytic and leadership skills. With a business under pressure, the leader must communicate with stakeholders in the enterprise including employees, customers, suppliers, shareholder, and banks so that they understand the timing and scope of the turnaround plan.

Within business lore, there are many famous turnaround figures, such as:

Jack Welch, at General Electric. Over a four year period from 1981 through 1985 Welch cut 100,000 jobs and earned the moniker Neutron Jack after the nuclear bomb that destroys people but leaves buildings standing. When Welch became CEO of GE, the company had 300 separate businesses, but beginning in the early 1980s Welch mandated that GE would only remain in those businesses where it was ranked first or second. By 1985, billions of dollars had been saved and the company restructured.

Louis Gerstner at IBM. When Louis Gerstner became CEO of IBM in 1993, many industry observers predicted its demise as a single entity. Big Blue, the inventor of the PC, the lifeblood of mainframe computing, was in disarray. Enter Gerstner, an outsider having come from RJR Nabisco and American Express Travel Related Services. As the *Boston Globe* noted when Gerstner took over at IBM, the nation's largest maker of computers, the company had "lost more than $16 billion in the previous four years while witnessing dramatic decline in market share, product leadership, and quite frankly, economic relevance." When Gerstner left IBM in 2003 the company had enjoyed seven consecutive years of profit and IBM's stock price had risen tenfold.

In creating the turnaround, Gerstner acted boldly, aggressively cutting prices in mainframes to regain market share, selling off assets to raise cash, and massively reengineering the company to cut costs and increase productivity. Since Gerstner's departure another, quieter turnaround occurred at IBM. In the pre-Gerstner era, IBM had been the king of product development; during the Gerstner era it turned to services to drive that turnaround; and since services stalled Big Blue has become increasingly reliant on software sales—in 2006, 40 percent of IBM's earnings came from software as IBM under a new leader has reinvented itself again.

Dick Brown at EDS. According to an article by Bill Breen in *Fast Company* ("How EDS Got Its Groove Back," October 1, 2001), when Brown took over at EDS in January 1999, he "joined a company that was floundering in a world it had created. EDS had pioneered the IT-services industry—the fastest growing industry in the world." But by 1996 it was "too slow for the fast-forward IT marketplace." Yet by the end of July 2001 EDS had increased its quarterly profits by 17 percent, saw a 7.5 percent rise in revenue, and had an $80 billion backlog of signed contracts.

For many the EDS turnaround demonstrates the importance of culture in creating change. Again according to *Fast Company*, "Brown quickly signaled that he would not put up with the old culture of information hoarding and rampant individualism. In one of his first meetings, Brown moved swiftly to change old beliefs and behaviors at EDS, unleashing a set of practices—dubbed 'operating mechanisms'—that were designed to create a company-wide culture based on instant feedback and direct, unfiltered communication." Changing the norms in how business got done at EDS was critical to its turnaround success.

Not all turnarounds are successful, nor their leaders famous. One infamous example is that of "Chainsaw Al Dunlop." As *BusinessWeek* noted on July 6, 1998, Dunlap arrived at Sunbeam (the appliance manufacturer) with sales of $1.2 million in July 1996. "Six months earlier, he had successfully completed the sale of Scott Paper Co. Less than four months later, Dunlap lived up to his reputation as a corporate demolition expert. He announced the shutdown or sale of two-thirds of Sunbeam's eighteen plants and the elimination of half its 12,000 employees." Yet the turnaround did not arrive. Ultimately, Dunlap was padding sales with abnormally high inventory levels and accounts receivable. He was subsequently fired by the board that had appointed him.

See also: Best Practice; Crisis/Risk Management; Downsizing

Further Reading

"Masters of Disaster," by Regina Fazio Maruca, *Fast Company* magazine (March 2001, Issue 45, Page 81).

24/7

As the numbers imply, the term "24/7" means twenty-four hours a day, seven days a week. Although it is now commonly used, the term reportedly originated within the IT industry, from its need to keep systems up and running, while providing technological support around the clock.

Now, though, the term has left the bailiwick of IT far behind. Customers expect to be able to shop, or get all sorts of information or help from companies at any hour they desire. And this means that the IT employees are not the only ones who have to be up and available "24/7." All types of businesses—at least those who work in customer service—are expected to be available around the clock.

The following passage was written by Anna Muoio for the September

1999 issue of *Fast Company* magazine (issue 28, page 72) and highlights the 24/7 world operating around us.

> The 7-Eleven store isn't the only place in Boynton Beach, Florida that's open all night. So is the human-resources department of Motorola's fast-paced manufacturing plant. Up in St. Cloud, Minnesota, Fingerhut (one of the world's largest direct marketers) offers a car-starting service for night-shift employees . . .

Though Muoio's article was written several years ago, it seems we have not slowed down since then. This is your wake-up call: The night shift isn't just for power-plant operators and assembly-line workers anymore. It's also for software developers, web producers, stockbrokers, and customer-service reps. The sun never sets on knowledge work and the new economy is open for business, twenty-four hours a day, seven days a week."

In her article, Muoio talked about twenty-four-hour child care centers and employees who dance around in the middle of the night to keep themselves awake. She also went on to quote Martin Moore-Ede, MD, who is the author of a book called *The Twenty-Four-Hour Society: Understanding Human Limits in a World That Never Stops* (Addison-Wesley, 1993). Moore-Ede, according to Muoio, said that most companies don't cope with the twenty-four-hour society very well. They staff up, but it's a "brute-force" approach, and employees over time "get run ragged." Moore-Ede also said, "There is a craziness to the 24-by-7 world," admits Moore-Ede who adds, "Just because it's possible doesn't mean that it's smart."

Moore-Ede's statements ring all too true. Consider the fire service, where some outdated fire and rescue departments in the United States still require dispatchers to work twenty-four-hour shifts, with only minimal breaks. Dispatchers are the people who answer the phone when people call in with an emergency; they also document and help coordinate the response. If you're a firefighter, or a member of the rescue squad, doing a twenty-four-hour shift generally means you can sleep—in between "calls." In and around your work duties, you can also move around, prepare a meal, exercise, or watch TV. In most departments, dispatchers, too, get regular breaks. But in some unfortunate venues, they're "on" almost the entire time and 24/7 is taken to an extreme.

> ### Why I Do This: Founder & CEO, Global Marketing Firm
> ### Paige Arnof-Fenn
>
> I am an entrepreneur and business owner, I founded a global marketing firm to help companies grow and succeed by reaching more customers in relevant ways. I started my firm by accident really so sometimes I tell people I am an accidental entrepreneur. I started my career in finance and then worked for several big companies before going to small firms and then founding my own business. I learned a lot in every job but this one is my favorite, I love the autonomy and flexibility of being your own boss, but I think I am better having worked for many tough bosses along the way to learn the ropes.
>
> I worked hard before but I have never worked harder in my life than I do now working for myself. If you like to push yourself and see what you can really do without the safety net of a big firm around you, then you will probably like a more entrepreneurial path too. You have to have a clear vision and a genuine passion, a good sense of humor, and a lot of energy to succeed. It is not for everyone but for those who have that entrepreneurial spirit and attitude, you will never be happy unless you follow your dreams one day, trust me. When you spend your time thinking about your idea and trying to figure out ways to execute it because you have to, not because someone is paying you or telling you to, you have been bitten by the bug too so embrace it and see where the path takes you. For me, it has been an incredible journey and I would not trade my experience for anything.

So is 24/7 a good thing? Well, ultimately, the success or failure of a 24/7 work environment probably depends on how the business handles the phenomenon. In the "new economy," customers are increasingly expecting to be able to do things like banking or shopping whenever they want to, regardless of the hour. Companies that want to meet those expectations need to find out how to do so—and how to ensure that tired or cranky employees aren't the norm when the business is going around the clock.

They might look to companies that have long been operating globally, for examples. Dealing with time changes created something akin to 24/7 within the international business community long before 24/7 became the buzzword it is as of this writing. Those pioneering IT departments who first came up with the term might be another good source of information. One thing's fairly certain: 24/7, or "anytime" is rapidly being joined by "anywhere" in the world of work. Maybe that's why, along with 24/7, there's also increased interest in terms like "work/family balance," "being unplugged," and "downtime."

Further Reading

"Are you Sure You're Up for the 24-hour Economy?" by Anna Muoio, *Fast Company* (September 1999), p. 72.

Signs of Changing Culture: Reluctant Vacationers: Why Americans Work More, Relax Less, than Europeans

Published: July 26, 2006 in Knowledge@Wharton

Reproduced with permission from Knowledge@Wharton (http://knowledge.wharton.upenn.edu), the online research and business analysis journal of the Wharton School of the University of Pennsylvania.

Beware, Lonely Planet Publications tells readers of its guide to France: This country largely closes down for the month of August. In Paris, particularly, shops are shuttered, and even some museums operate for only limited hours. Locals seem to migrate—en masse—to vacation resorts along the Atlantic Coast and the Riviera.

The French and, for that matter, people in much of the rest of Western Europe, can afford to check out for a month because they receive an average of nearly two months a year in paid leave, a combination of vacation and government holidays, according to the Organisation for Economic Co-operation and Development. That distinguishes them from citizens of the United States, who, despite a similarly productive economy and a comparable standard of living, enjoy about half as much paid time off. The average American receives approximately four weeks a year of paid leave, while the average person in France gets seven and the average German, eight.

Sure, plenty of Americans will take a vacation next month. If you have ever spent an hour in August sweltering in the lines at Disney World or stuck in the traffic on New York's Long Island Expressway, you know that. But Europeans, with their generous allowances of downtime, can afford to loll around for the whole month, not just the one week that's typical in the United States.

Work and vacation habits in the world's most economically advanced regions weren't always this way. As recently as the 1960s, Europeans worked more than people in the United States, according to a 2005 study by Bruce Sacerdote of Dartmouth University and Alberto Alesina and Ed Glaeser, both of Harvard University. Since then, however, the regions' appetites for leisure have diverged, with Americans grinding away for ever-more hours at the office and Europeans taking time to savor *la dolce vita* ("the sweet life"). These days, the United States even outworks famously industrious Japan.

Curse of the Blackberry

What changed? The explanations vary as much as the potential locales for a summer sojourn. Several experts at Wharton see a role for culture and history. A Nobel laureate, in contrast, says the difference boils down to taxes. And Sacerdote, Alesina, and Glaeser chalk it up to levels of unionization.

Cultural explanations enjoy the most currency in the popular press. In the United States, publications like the *Wall Street Journal* brag about the productivity and work ethic of big-shouldered America, while European commentators sniff about what fun-hating grinds Americans have become. These are obviously caricatures, but they do appear to hold some truth, scholars at Wharton say. Europeans seem to place a higher value on leisure, while Americans tend to prefer earning and spending. As a result, Americans on average own bigger cars, bigger houses and more vacation homes, says Witold Rybczynski, a Wharton real estate professor.

In contrast, Europeans' self worth is often tied up not with whether they drive a Lexus or a Porsche but with their ability to enjoy a hefty holiday, says Mauro Guillen, Wharton management and sociology professor and a native of Spain. "It is a sign of social status in Europe to take a long vacation away from home. Money is not everything in Europe; status is not only conferred by money. Having fun, or being able to have fun, also is a sign of success and a source of social esteem."

Likewise, Christian Schneider, manager of the multinational research advisory group at the Wharton Center for Human Resources, points out that European managers often use all of their vacation time, even as their U.S. counterparts brag about their workaholism. "There's a tendency to really relax in Europe, to disengage from work," says Schneider, a native of Germany. "When an American finally does take those few days of vacation per year, they are most likely to be in constant contact with the office." Call it the curse of the Blackberry.

This cultural chasm can surprise Europeans who come to work in the United States. Denise Dahlhoff, a director for Wharton Executive Education, remembers seeing her vacation days cut nearly in half when she took a job in the New Jersey office of ACNielsen, a market-research company. The consultancy she had worked for in Bonn, Germany, gave her 25 days a year—five days more than the minimum required by German law—while Nielsen initially provided only 10. (The United States has no statutory minimum.) She also learned that, unlike many Germans, Americans typically check their e-mails even when they leave the office for just a couple of days. "It's definitely socially more acceptable to take vacation in Germany," she says. "Taking two or three weeks off without being in touch is fine."

Cultural differences undoubtedly exist, but for Ed Prescott, a Nobel Prize-winning economist at Arizona State University, they don't explain something as basic as work habits. He instead credits taxes. In a 2003 study, Prescott points out that European countries have much higher marginal tax rates than the United States. As a result, he argues, Europeans have much less incentive to work additional hours. Why plug away for 45 hours, instead of 37.5, when the government ends up taking much of your extra income?

Peter Cappelli, a Wharton management professor and director of the school's Center for Human Resources, doesn't buy that argument. Marginal tax rates don't really apply to salaried workers, who are paid a set amount no matter how long they work and are taxed accordingly. And it's these people, not hourly employees, who have lately seen the biggest gains in hours worked, he says.

In addition, many surveys have shown that Americans are willing to accept less money for more vacation, he notes. Even so, their hours keep creeping higher. "People here are working more than they want to because that's cheaper for employers than hiring new employees," he adds. "In the U.S., there isn't much of a way for employees to rebel against that. Unions only represent a small proportion of people, and they are mostly blue collar."

Unions' Clout

Sacerdote, Alesina, and Glaeser's analysis mirrors Cappelli's. They, too, conclude that different levels of unionization explain why Europeans work so much less than Americans these days. Simply put, burlier European unions bargained for more vacation. About nine out of 10 workers in Germany and France are covered by collective-bargaining agreements, compared with only about two of 10 in the United States, they point out. Because of their heft, European unions have more muscle in politics and board rooms. As a consequence, they succeed at lobbying for policies that benefit their members and employees in general. In contrast, political decisions in the United States tend to favor employers.

Yet that argument still seems to leave room for a greater European liking for leisure; after all, European unions could have fought for higher pay, not more vacation. Sacerdote, Alesina, and Glaeser say that expediency, not a cultural predisposition for kicking back, drove their decisions.

In the 1970s, Western Europe's economy endured a series of economic shocks, including the oil crisis, they explain. In response, employers insisted that they needed to lay off workers. Unions, in turn, proposed retaining workers but cutting everyone's hours. The outcome would be the same—a reduction in total hours and thus costs—but it would achieve savings without layoffs. These "work-sharing" arrangements were often promoted with slogans like "work less; work all," the professors write.

"Work sharing may make little sense as a national response to a negative economic shock," they add. "But at a single firm, a membership-maximizing union may indeed find work sharing to be an attractive policy."

Once work hours started falling for large numbers of Europeans, a "social multiplier" kicked in; more people wanted more vacation because their family and friends were getting it. People enjoy taking time off together, even if it means inconveniencing themselves to do so. "We put ourselves through a lot of pain to standardize on things like our weekends and our vacations because there are big complementarities," Sacerdote says. Even in America, you can see the hassles that this tendency causes: Home Depot wouldn't be so jammed on Saturday mornings if most people didn't have the same days off each week.

Regardless of who's right in the debate, these differences in work habits may not endure. Faced with slow-growing economies and social unrest stemming from youth unemployment, some European politicians have begun to jawbone for change. And corporate managers there have begun to squeeze more flexible work rules out of unions, including longer hours and fewer restrictions on firing, by threatening to move plants abroad. Just this week, the *Wall Street Journal* documented how, in response to these sorts of changes, some German firms have stepped up hiring at home. If this trend continues, it might not only jumpstart Western Europe's economies but also begin to increase average work hours and decrease paid holidays.

Sacerdote agrees that labor restrictions play a role in Europe's higher levels of unemployment. Policies that make employment costly—like lots of paid leave and restrictions on hiring—can also make employers reluctant to hire. But he also sees a "bedrock issue" that no amount of negotiating will solve. "Labor is so much less mobile in Europe," he points out. "So when Ireland is booming, it's not like people pour out of France into Ireland. Even within Germany, you have high unemployment in East Germany, yet people don't move west. In the U.S., it's labor mobility that helps the labor market. But people don't just pick up and move in Europe."

Undergirding the debate about vacation is the unstated premise that "more is better." Besides the occasional Scrooge-like boss, everybody loves vacation—or at least says they do—and attests to its usefulness as a way for workers to recharge.

But count Nancy Rothbard, a Wharton management professor, among the rare skeptics. She cites research that has found that the recharge effect lasts about three days. And for many people, those three days come with a hefty price of their own—and it's not entirely financial. "Would more vacation be better for us?" she asks. "It depends on the tradeoffs." If it means making less money, some people might pass, preferring to save for their children's college educations, their retirements or even a house at the beach—even if they rarely have the time to use it.

Studies also show that some people bank weeks and weeks of vacation, she points out. Analysts tend to assume that their bosses discourage them from taking their time or that they fear a rock pile of work when they return. But it's possible that they just don't want to leave work.

Consider parents, she says. Hauling kids on long trips can be more stressful than staying at home. If people can afford to bring along grandparents or babysitters, then they can still rest and relax. If they can't, working may beat refereeing backseat boxing matches in the mini-van. What's more, vacations, especially with gas prices at $3 a gallon and airfares rising, aren't cheap. "It takes a lot of resources to vacation with a family. Not everybody can afford to go to Paris."

Besides, if they go there in August, they might find all the shops closed.

Value Proposition

Every company that sells something to customers has a value proposition—the way in which it adds unique value as compared to its competitors. When customers choose to buy from a company, they buy into the value proposition of that company consciously or subconsciously, choosing your points of differentiation in the product or its services. For example, customers that purchase food from McDonald's buy into its value proposition—inexpensive, standardized food, served quickly. A customer that purchases a Dell computer is subscribing to another value proposition—customized computers at reasonable prices, but without the ability to see the machine in advance of purchase. Volvo's value proposition is based on the reliability and proven safety of its cars as opposed to cutting edge design.

In "Customer Value Propositions in Business Markets" (*Harvard Business Review*, March 2006), the authors suggest three generic types of value propositions:

All benefits. This value proposition is simply the list of all the benefits a company believes that its offering might deliver to target customers. There are pitfalls to this approach that include claiming advantages for features that have limited or no value for the target market and "that many, even most, of the benefits may be points of parity with those of the next best alternative, diluting the effect of the few genuine points of difference."

Favorable points of difference. This type of value proposition explicitly recognizes that the customer has an alternative. As the authors point out, this type of value proposition answers the question "Why should our firm purchase your offering instead of your competitor's?" which is a more pertinent question than "Why should I buy your product?" Yet, "knowing that an element of an offering is a point of difference relative to the next best alternative does not, however, convey the value of this difference to target customers. Furthermore, a product or service may have several points of difference, complicating the supplier's understanding of which ones deliver the greatest value."

Resonating focus. The authors suggest that "the resonating focus value proposition should be the gold standard" for value propositions, noting that "this type of proposition differs from favorable points of difference in two significant respects. First, more is not better. Although a supplier's offering may possess several favorable points of difference, the resonating focus proposition steadfastly concentrates on the one or two points of difference that deliver, and whose improvement will continue to deliver, the greatest value to target customers. . . . Second, the resonating focus proposition may contain a point of parity."

While value propositions are most readily associated with customers and marketing, they have begun to be used in other business applications. For example, in a recent book entitled *The HR Value Proposition* (Harvard Business School Press, 2005) the authors argue that human resources departments need to take on the notion of value, earn a seat at the executive table based on value, and be able to answer the question "Why should I listen to you?"

See also: Competitive Advantage; Relationship Marketing

Further Reading

The Core Value Proposition: Capture the Power of Your Business Building Ideas, by Jack G. Hardy, Trafford Publishing (July 6, 2006).

Virtual Teams

If a large amount of individuals were asked to define the word team, most would come up with a similar answer—a group working together toward a common goal. As examples you'll get innumerable sports references: baseball teams, football teams, etc. Indeed, working together to win games is a basic premise of any so-called "team sport."

Teams have an important function in business as well, and have for decades. Groups of employees are often set up to oversee development or marketing of a specific product; for instance, video games are often developed by a team within a company rather than everyone who works there (e.g., at Sega, the Sonic Team is the group working on, among other things, the extremely successful Sonic the Hedgehog franchise).

Until roughly fifteen years ago, teams worked together both mentally and physically, with members present in a single location, though occasionally a member might be "present" on the phone. But beginning in the 1990s, with globalization and the need to be present to customers and suppliers on a 24/7 basis, virtual teams began to develop. Team members were scattered across the globe, yet worked together on a variety of tasks that included developing projects, managing customer service, or crafting a strategic plan for the organization. This allowed companies to reach far and wide to utilize the most skilled employees on any team worldwide, and to have team meetings "on the spot" whenever trouble or deadlines made a meeting necessary—and without paying for the airfare or wasting time gathering the team together.

While setting up virtual teams is new for some organizations, others have been organizing and running virtual teams for many years. As *Training Strategies for Tomorrow* ("Nortel and BP Succeed through Virtual Teamwork," May/June 2002, p. 3) noted:

For BP, virtual teamwork is relatively old hat. They have been employing this technique as far back as 1994 and to good effect. For example, in 1995, work on a North Sea drilling ship ground to a halt due to equipment failure. Because the workers on board could not ascertain the cause of the problem, they were faced with the prospect of taking the ship back to port. Not an appealing option when the leasing cost was $150,000 a day! Fortunately for the crew, they were currently participating in a BP pilot project called "Virtual teamwork"—all they had to do was show the faulty machinery to an on-shore expert through a video satellite link-up which had recently been installed on the ship. The expert was then able to diagnose the problem, thus enabling work to continue in a relatively short space of time and saving BP thousands of dollars.

The same article identifies challenges in developing high performance virtual teams. Some of them are the same problems as in "in-person" teams, including interpersonal issues between members, a lack of trust, and in some cases difficulty using the technology designed to support the team. Other concerns are ineffective communication (much of communication is non-verbal), lack of leisure time (as virtual teams can meet at any time), security concerns (much of the work product is online and vulnerable to hacking), over-emphasis on speed, and too many members (it is tempting to keep adding people).

See also: Internet; Intranet/Extranet; Networking; Telework

Further Reading

Mastering Virtual Teams: Strategies, Tools, and Techniques That Succeed (Jossey Bass Business and Management Series), by Debrah L. Duarte and Nancy Tennant Snyder, Jossey-Bass, 3rd ed. (April 21, 2006).

War for Talent

In the current climate, businesses have begun to realize that the competition for talented employees has become worldwide, and has in fact become so competitive it is nothing short of a war between companies for the talent to keep them not only afloat but moving into the future.

On October 7, 2006, *The Economist* article "Survey: The Battle for Brainpower" put this "War for Talent" into perspective,

> In a speech at Harvard University in 1943 Winston Churchill observed that "the empires of the future will be empires of the mind." He might have added that the battles of the future will be battles for talent. To be sure, the old battles for natural resources are still with us. But they are being supplemented by new ones for talent—not just among companies (which are competing for "human resources") but also among countries (which fret about the "balance of brains" as well as the "balance of power").
>
> The war for talent is at its fiercest in high-tech industries. The arrival of an aggressive new superpower—Google—has made it bloodier still. The company has assembled a formidable hiring machine to help it find the people it needs. It has also experimented with clever new recruiting tools, such as billboards featuring complicated mathematical problems.

With the wave of job losses in the post-Internet bubble, the idea of a battle for talent seems remote or even far-fetched. Yet, the problem is real. As *Fast Company* noted on August 1, 1998 in "The War for Talent," a lot of it has to do with demographics. In fifteen years, there will be 15 percent fewer Americans in the 35–45-year-old range than there are now. At the same time, the U.S. economy is likely to grow at a rate of 3 percent to 4 percent per year. So over that period, the demand for bright, talented 35–45-year-olds will increase by, say, 25 percent, and the supply will be going down by 15 percent. That sets the stage for a talent war.

Why I Do This: Divorce Mediator and Lawyer
Susan Matthew

My job is to help divorcing people resolve their differences, solve their problems, and obtain a divorce through a process that is less time-consuming, emotionally easier, and less expensive than divorce litigation. In order to explain what divorce mediation is, I have to first explain what it isn't, and it isn't divorce *litigation*. In divorce litigation, divorcing couples each hire lawyers and the lawyers and the couples may argue for years over many different issues in the divorce, from deciding how the property will be divided to deciding who will have custody of the kids, sometimes asking a judge to make the decision for them. In divorce mediation, the couples make the decisions themselves, with my help. I sit with the couples and help them to talk through their concerns and come up with possible solutions to their problems. My job is to be neutral. I don't offer any advice and I don't make the decisions, but I help the people who are divorcing have conversations with one another so they can come up with their own answers to their own problems. Mediators spend a lot of time listening to people in order to help them solve their problems. Sometimes I write down exactly what people say to help me explain to the other person how or why the person is feeling the way that he or she does. I always tell people that my job is to help people have a conversation with each other and to help people figure out what they really want in their divorce.

My typical day involves talking to people on the telephone and explaining divorce mediation to them, meeting with couples for a few hours at a time in a mediation session, and writing up legal agreements, which document the agreement reached in a mediation session. I work in an office and use the telephone and computer.

I like my job because I went to law school to learn to help people. After being a divorce lawyer for many years, I decided to stop fighting cases and start mediating them instead. I like the mediation process because it helps me to be creative, and it helps me to use my natural skills at listening and understanding people. I would recommend this job to someone who is good at listening to other people, who is good at coming up with creative solutions, and who likes problem solving, talking, thinking, and writing. Being a mediator is not a good job for someone who wants to be the boss in a situation. If you are the problem-solver in your family, you are probably already a mediator!

More recent evidence is the number of companies expanding their human resources function to seek out new people and to upgrade the skills of current employees. In 2005, "2,300 firms adopted some form of talent-management technology—and the status and size of human-resource departments have risen accordingly. These days Goldman Sachs has a 'university,' McKinsey has a 'people committee' and Singapore's Ministry of Manpower has an international talent division." ("The Search for Talent," *The Economist*, October 7, 2006).

Moreover, the solution in the war for talent cannot be found in developing countries. Despite the number of "high-talent" work that has been outsourced to China and India, these countries themselves have found increasing shortages of capable people. Nor will the war for talent only be found in engineering and high-tech; experts predict that there will be a substantive shortage of skilled people across all occupations.

See also: Headhunter

Further Reading

Managing Across Cultures, by Susan C. Schneider and Jean-Louis Barsoux, Prentice Hall, 2nd ed. (December 3, 2002).

The War for Talent, by Ed Michaels, Helen Handfield-Jones, and Beth Axelrod, Harvard Business School Press (October 2001).

Water Cooler

Traditionally, the water cooler was just that, a place where people went to get a glass of cold water on their breaks. It was also a gathering place where employees could speak informally about a range of issues from the home team's performance in the football game to actions going on in the organization.

For some the water cooler talk symbolizes "real" communication among ordinary workers broken down without corporate spin. It is informal, without the need for political or organizational correctness. It is a place to create the community that brings an organization together. In the opinion of others, however, water cooler conversations are little more than gossip and rumor mongering about perceived slights, promotions, and layoffs. As a result, companies generally try to keep sensitive information from becoming fodder for water cooler conversation lest it become distorted and harmful to the organization.

More recently the water cooler has been less of a natural gathering place—today especially there are fewer communal breaks and more beverage options contributing to the decline of the water cooler as a gathering place. However, the need to gather and informally communicate has not gone away. Other physical locations have taken the place of the water cooler. These include the printer; generally employees do not have a dedicated personal printer and as a result congregate waiting to pick up their print jobs. Another location is the office kitchen, which acts as a site for community development as well. There is also the "smoker's area," where employees that smoke gather to indulge their habits. What is interesting about these "new" water coolers is the democratic nature of the groups. In the informal "smoker's" water cooler, one would be equally likely to find junior clerks and executive vice presidents, all drawn together by their habit and exchanging conversations on a variety of topics from business to sports and families.

As the Internet has come into prominence the "new age" water cooler has emerged—e-mail and "blogs" have become the proxy for the water cooler. But the medium has its problems. For example, a study in the *Journal of Personality and Social Psychology* found that emotion and tone are not always conveyed in e-mail. What a sender thinks is funny may not be received as such by the recipients because it does not have the associated body language or vocal clues. Also, unfortunately some employees believed that these electronic communications sites were a secure place where people could privately exchange views. In some cases, these views were brought to the attention of the company and resulted in employees being let go. Especially in the case of e-mail communication there is no presumption that the communication is private. Indeed Apple, Delta Airlines, Google, Microsoft, and Starbucks have dismissed employees over blog content

Still, water cooler blogging can also have a positive effect. An Edelman/Intelliseek survey found that bloggers were twice as likely to put their job in a positive light than they were to denigrate it.

Whether it be "live" or through an electronic medium, the need for the water cooler remains strong. Studies have shown that the "water cooler" chat creates meaningful bonds and sense of community that improves productivity and spurs innovation. Additionally such a sense of belonging offers an antidote to the problem of retention. Employees with a sense of belonging and connection with their co-workers are less likely to leave— and the companies that employ them are more likely to benefit from the training and investment made in the employees.

See also: Horizontal Organizations; Suggestion Box

Further Reading

The Corporate Culture Handbook: How to Plan, Implement, And Measure a Successful Culture Change Programme, by Gabrielle O'Donovan, Liffey Press (June 30, 2006).

60 People to Avoid at the Water Cooler, by Josh Aiello, Broadway (August 24, 2004).

Whistleblower

To understand the meaning of a whistleblower, it helps to think about a sporting event. When a foul is committed the referee blows the whistle. In organizations, especially in business and government, people are called whistleblowers when they blow the whistle on improprieties. According to a column by Nancy Cooper, located in the Inc. magazine online resource center, "Originally, the term 'whistleblower' referred to employees who reported, or attempted to report, fraud in government contracts. However, as the statutes have evolved, the term has also been attached to protections for any employee trying to exercise various rights under labor statutes or working to protect the public interest."

In recent years, there have been many high profile cases of whistleblowers, some of which have been the subject of books and movies. These include:

- **Karen Silkwood**. The movie *Silkwood,* starring Meryl Streep, Kurt Russell, and Cher, tells the story of Karen Silkwood, a famous whistleblower and a chemical technician at the Kerr–McGee's plutonium fuels production plant in Crescent, Oklahoma. She was a union member and activist who was critical of plant safety. Shortly after providing the Atomic Energy Commission with a list of violations at the plant, Silkwood died in a car accident, fueling some speculation that she had been forced off the road. In the week prior to her death, Silkwood was reportedly gathering evidence for the

Why I Do This: Vice President/Senior Sales Officer
Treasury Services for Investment Bank
Carol Perrault*

I have just entered Corporate Finance after many years of sales experience in a variety of industries (telecommunications, fitness, luxury goods, consumer finance). My most recent sales experience of five years with a major consumer credit and finance company prompted my interest in corporate finance.

To prepare myself for this desired transition and to have the best chance of success once in a corporate finance role, I took two years while also working to complete my Executive MBA. With an undergraduate degree in English, I believe an MBA would be useful and ultimately necessary as an industry "door-opener." Two of the most practical skills that I needed to make a career change were provided by a graduate business degree—quantitative foundations for financial decision-making and an overall strategic business orientation for assessing opportunities, risks, and framing decisions.

My job is in Treasury Services for a major bank. Treasury Services handles the core cash management needs of middle to large corporate businesses (small business is usually adequately served by retail banking products).

Core cash management involves business needs for payment, collection, liquidity, investment management, and trade finance. Treasury products include sweep accounts, cash deposit and overnight rates, commercial credit, accounts receivable/payable management, retail and wholesale lockbox services, supply chain financing, ACH debit and Fed wire originations, commercial card (corporate card/purchasing card), and US Dollar Clearing.

Specifically, I sell (working with a Treasury team) four account receivables management products to mid-large corporate clients that seek to accelerate the posting of their receivables. This is accomplished primarily through electronic payment channels. My employer bank holds nine patents for check imaging, collections, and supply chain financing.

In working with a team, I sell both internally and externally. A treasury officer "owns" an account in terms of overall relationship and then I am brought in when specific products are needed. At that point, I am selling externally—communicating the features, benefits, and the value proposition of my products relative to its price to the prospective client.

I like my job because it offers me the opportunity to learn a lot about the corporate finance industry from one of the top players in the field. The breadth and resources of the bank also provides me with the ability in the future to hopefully get into some different areas of banking I am most interested in (M&A work).

Day-to-day, I enjoy learning from intelligent people who similarly like what they are doing and have industry know-how. Most peers and colleagues are forward-thinkers and team players—doing what needs to be done, and doing it well. And, of course, I enjoy the pace, multi-tasking, and strategic thinking involved in a complex, long term cycle sales process.

What would someone find "unexpected" about my job? How complex it really is, but smart, talented people make it look simple—one reason why remuneration in this field can be highly criticized.

Why would you recommend it?

It is fun (for those who like puzzles), never boring (for good or bad!), and you can pay your bills doing this.

What kind of person might enjoy doing your kind of job?

Driven, ambitious, competitive, problem-solvers, strategic thinkers, must like many moving parts.

*Name changed for privacy.

---

union to support her claim that Kerr–McGee was negligent in maintaining plant safety, yet at the same time she was involved in a number of unexplained exposures to plutonium.

- **Deep Throat**. For many, Deep Throat is the ultimate whistleblower from the government sector. Keeping his identity secret, Deep Throat provided insider guidance to reporters from *The Washington Post* newspaper, exposing the Watergate scandal and resulting in the resignation of then-president Richard M. Nixon on August 9, 1974. Deep Throat's identity remained secret for thirty years until it was revealed in 2005 as W. Mark Felt, a high ranking official in the FBI. Meeting in secret locations, Deep Throat unveiled the web of internal spies, secret surveillance, and political "dirty tricks" that were part of the Watergate scandal. The reporters' story became the best-selling memoir *All the President's Men*, and two years later in 1976 became a movie of the same name that prominently featured Deep Throat.
- **Jeffrey Winguard**. In 1989, Winguard was recruited to Brown and Williamson Tobacco Corp. to develop a safer cigarette. Although the program was scrapped, he discovered that the company not only knew its products were addictive; they also used additives that they knew caused health risks. Not long after bringing the matter to the attention of the CEO, Winguard was dismissed. In 1995 he played a significant role in blowing the whistle on the tobacco companies, leading to a $246 billion settlement between tobacco companies and forty-six states that sued companies to recoup medical costs from illnesses associated with smoking.

For many, 2002 was the Year of the Whistleblower when *Time* magazine selected three high-profile whistleblowers as its Persons of the Year. They were Sherron Watkins, a former vice-president of Enron who wrote a letter to that company's CEO warning of improper accounting methods; Colleen Rowley, an FBI staff attorney who revealed that the FBI director had ignored her request for assistance in investigating what would ultimately become one of the 9/11 terrorists; and Cynthia Cooper, who informed the WorldCom's board that the company had improperly covered up almost $4 billion in losses. That publicity has created increased scrutiny of organizations.

As a former federal prosecutor who represents whistleblowers noted in *BusinessWeek* (December 16, 2002), a "do the right thing" culture has developed in which people believe they must ring the alarm when they suspect wrong-doing—even if there are high personal costs. Notably it has "recast whistleblowers from crackpots to national champions."

As might be expected, whistleblowers are often unpopular in their own organizations and historically have been dismissed, discredited, and blackballed. The U.S. Department of Labor, through the Occupational Safety and Health Administration, protects whistleblowers from discrimination and investigates claims that whistleblowers have been terminated, demoted, and/or harassed. Additionally, under the Sarbanes–Oxley legislation, whistleblowers only need to make a disclosure to a supervisor, law-enforcement agency, or congressional investigator that could have a material impact on a company's shares.

See also: Code of Ethics

Further Reading

Whistleblowers: Broken Lives and Organizational Power, by C. Fred Alford, Cornell University Press (February 2002).

White Collar

The term "white collar" came into use during the industrialization of U.S. business. Generally speaking "white collar" workers were literally that—workers who wore "white shirts" (with white collars) and ties, and carried a brief case. They were characterized as the managerial and professional class. By contrast, blue collar workers were factory and trades people who carried lunch boxes. Both were members of the middle class, with the white collar worker generally seen as part of the upper middle class and the blue collar workers the lower middle class.

The rise of unions further identified the struggle as between the white collar "management" and the blue collar "worker." Over time a series of attributes became associated with white collar workers. They were better paid, better educated, and worked in clean, comfortable offices. Blue collar workers were paid by the hour, had high school diplomas, and worked in the dangerous conditions present on the factory floor. Indeed, the cultural attributes of both groups created a virtual "caste" system, with white collar workers at the top and blue collar workers at the bottom.

Beginning in the 1970s, some saw white collar workers as a contributing factor to the decline in the competitiveness of U.S. manufacturing, especially in the auto industry. White collar workers were typified as sitting in offices, drawing big salaries, and making decisions divorced from the realities of the shop floor where the business of manufacturing really happened. The rise of the Japanese automakers seemed to further illustrate this point. While U.S. white collar workers were isolated from the manufacturing line, their Japanese and to some extent German counterparts actively sought out the feedback from their blue collar work forces. Process improvements, vital to improvements in quality and prices, came about through the interaction of the white and blue collar workers. In the United States, however, with its historically adversarial relationship between the white collar and blue collar workers, there was a greater emphasis on automation that would reduce the size of the blue collar work force.

As the manufacturing sector declined in the United States, white collar workers became more prevalent but their status generally diminished, as so many people fell within the category. White collar workers were office workers, middle managers, and IT workers rather than rising executives. Traditionally, white collar workers were paid by the month based on an annual salary with no allowance for overtime. As the demand of the work increased, white collar workers worked longer hours with no extra pay, and there were suggestions that they would create a union. Outsourcing and downsizing attacked job stability such that white collar workers had to seek the protection of unions; several of the fastest growing unions in the United States at the time represented white collar workers (physicians, nuclear engineers, and psychologists). As the *Wall Street Journal* noted,

"American architects, radiologists, and tax accountants feel nervous about Indian competitors" (hence the white collar unions).

The traditionally strong differentiation between white collar and blue collar workers had political implications. Political strategists created plans to attract each group based on their defined attributes. Historically blue collar workers had been easier to reach. They were already organized through their unions and could be counted on to turn out in large numbers on election day.

Increasingly the lines between white collar and blue collar workers were blurring. White collar workers were becoming more plentiful and enjoyed less job security. As white collar workers moved "down," blue collar workers moved "up," with many traditionally blue collar jobs requiring advanced technology and electronics skills.

White Collar Crime

According to the FBI website, www.fbi.gov, "The term white collar crime was reportedly coined in 1939 by Professor Edwin Sutherland and has since become synonymous with the full range of frauds committed by business and government professionals. Today's con artists are more savvy and sophisticated than ever, engineering everything from slick online scams to complex stock and health care frauds."

According to the Legal Information Institute at Cornell Law School, white-collar offenses included: antitrust violations, computer and Internet fraud, credit card fraud, phone and telemarketing fraud, bankruptcy fraud, healthcare fraud, environmental law violations, insurance fraud, mail fraud, government fraud, tax evasion, financial fraud, securities fraud, insider trading, bribery, kickbacks, counterfeiting, public corruption, money laundering, embezzlement, economic espionage, and trade secret theft. The estimated cost to the United States was more than $300 billion annually. Penalties for white collar crime included fines, forfeitures, restitution, and imprisonment.

Some perceived white collar crime as a "victimless" crime, one without violence that did not result in harm. Yet, white collar crime did have victims—investors that lost retirement savings, increased cost of business operation that resulted in higher prices, and equally important an erosion of public trust. In comparison to other crimes, white collar crime was difficult to prove, as offenders were often highly skilled and adept at hiding their activities through a series of sophisticated transactions.

From the late 1980s through the present there have been several notorious incidences of white collar crime, including the 1989 indictment of Michael Milken, a renowned junk bond trader for securities fraud. More recently the scale of white collar crime in scandals such as Enron, Tyco, and Worldcom has epitomized corporate greed and corruption.

Beyond high profile business cases, white collar criminals are increasingly turning to technology to fuel their schemes. White collar criminals armed with computer skills are able to hack not only into financial institutions but also into personal records to "steal identities" for use in other fraudulent acts.

See also: Code of Ethics; Hacker; Whistleblower

Further Reading

The Organization Man, by William H. Whyte, University of Pennsylvania Press, New Ed ed. (May 2002).

White Collar: The American Middle Classes, by C. Wright Mills and Russell Jacoby, Oxford University Press, Fiftieth Anniversary Edition (August 13, 2002).

Appendix

Culture: A Force for Alignment

It's 2 A.M. on Sunday in New York, and a partner at a consulting firm is expecting a phone call from a colleague in Tokyo. He's going to be briefing her about a multinational consumer goods company he worked with two years ago. She'll be meeting with the company on Tuesday morning to pitch a long-term project.

The partner in New York is well prepared for the phone call. He took time on Friday to pull together a package of information—to review his experiences, to synthesize his knowledge. Time away from his current clients. Time away from selling new business. Personal time. For someone in Tokyo he barely knows. There's no rule book that says he has to do this, nor will he get any tangible reward.

The phone call lasts three hours. His colleague is grateful; he's glad he could help. The meeting on Tuesday goes well; the multinational signs on. The firm beats a direct competitor; the cash register rings.

It's 2 A.M. on Sunday in New York, and a partner at another consulting firm is sleeping. A colleague in Tokyo called him last week, asking for advice on a multinational client with whom she knew he had a great deal of experience. He spent fifteen minutes on the phone with her, giving her an overview. He didn't offer to do more; she didn't expect him to do more. Six years ago, he would have taken the time to be more helpful. But that was then; this is now. The firm isn't the same place it once was; it's every man for himself these days.

Two weeks later, the client takes its business elsewhere, saying in a letter that the competitor it has chosen to do business with is "better prepared to handle the needs of a growing, global company." The firm takes an imperceptible step toward mediocrity.

What's the critical difference between these two firms?

In a word: Culture.

Most people believe that culture is amorphous and intangible—something that exists and influences behavior at the margin, but certainly isn't strategic. They also believe that culture is something you inherit, rather than something you create and manage.

They're right—but only to a point. Culture is amorphous; it is intangible. But it *directly* affects the behavior of every single person in your organization. And it isn't simply inherited; it isn't just *there*. To borrow a quote from Shakespeare, "What's past is prologue." Culture is dynamic. And whether you know it or not, you *manage* it on a daily basis. You shape the culture of your firm by the decisions you make or facilitate, which then affect behavior, which subsequently becomes part of "how things are done here." You may be reinforcing the culture you inherited through your actions; you may also be breaking new ground, changing the culture of your firm, slightly or drastically, and significantly affecting your firm's competitive position as you do.

As we've seen, success has a price. Success can bring complexity—a larger firm, for example, and one that is operating all over the world. Success—and growth—can also bring a concomitant need for capital and

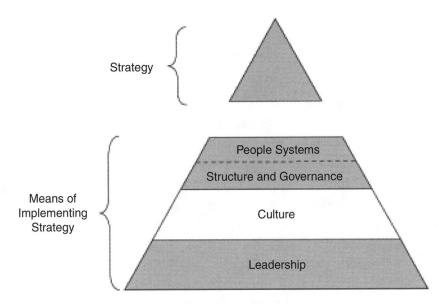

Figure A1 Alignment Pyramid: Culture

currency for paying stars, which may lead a private firm to go public. Changes like these inevitably threaten the strategic identity and alignment that have driven the firm's success. But the firms that endure through growing pains, changes in ownership, and other challenges manage their culture to minimize the stress of change. They turn to it as a support mechanism and as a rudder to remind them of their course in the face of new challenges. And they work to change it, as needed, to adapt to new circumstances (see Figure A1.)

What Is Culture?

Reduced to its essentials, *culture* is a system of beliefs that members of an organization share about the goals and values that are important to them and about the behavior that is appropriate to attain those goals and live those values. The concept of culture had its roots in anthropological studies in the early twentieth century. Social scientists used the term to refer to the persistent pattern of beliefs and customs they observed in their studies of South Pacific islanders, African bush dwellers, and American Indian tribes, among others. Several decades later, scholars interested in business organizations recognized that companies and firms also developed patterns of beliefs and customs, and that those beliefs and customs had a strong influence on how employees behaved. And so the concept was brought into the modern business vocabulary.

Culture encompasses beliefs about everything that goes on in a firm. Culture is never completely codified in a formal rule book or a policy manual. Instead it is a set of invisible guideposts that define how people should behave. It establishes the "dos"—what you are expected to do—and also the "don'ts"—what is implicitly prohibited—at levels ranging from the smallest of decisions (what to wear) to the largest (what line of business the firm is in, or whether to accept a certain client).

At Bain, for example—and this is a small thing, but telling—consultants are obsessive about communicating through voice mail. Messages are sent and received by hundreds of professionals every hour, from sites around the globe. People are expected to check voice mail on Saturdays, Sundays, and even over vacation. The practice isn't recorded in an employee handbook or taught in introductory training sessions. But everyone knows that they must remain connected, in real time, to case teams, colleagues, and clients. Memos are rare in Bain's fast-paced environment, and e-mail, while useful, is only a backup in its highly oral culture.

Hambrecht & Quist provides another good example. At H&Q, seasoned bankers routinely take associates with them to client meetings, spending time after the event to debrief. They explain why they approached the client *this* way. Why they didn't start the meeting *that* way. Why they reacted as they did when the client said *this*. Why they didn't offer *that* information. The practice isn't required by some written policy. It's not part of a formal training program. It's done because that's the way Hambrecht & Quist teaches its junior people the art of client management. It's done because "That's the way we do things here."

There's a tendency on the part of many top managers to believe that they can legislate behavior through edicts and devices such as job descriptions. (Think about the millions of dollars in money and time that have been spent on elaborate new organization charts and job descriptions that are expected to transform people's behavior.) The habit is understandable, given the industrial heritage of business. And in factory settings, where employees punch time clocks and work on assembly lines, it's natural that policy, procedure, and discipline shape behavior even today.

But in PSFs, where people have so much personal discretion and autonomy, culture has more influence on a professional's behavior than any job description or corporate policy ever written. Policies and procedures, manuals, and job descriptions cannot dictate behavior effectively where professionals work without close supervision, people are running their own offices and practices, partners are serving their own clients, and leadership is highly decentralized. Culture is a dominant force—if not *the* dominant force—in determining how the members of the firm actually behave toward one another and toward their clients. The greater the degree of freedom, the more important culture is in determining how an individual works.

Survival of the Culturally Fit

Unfortunately, there are no clear mortality rates for PSFs. Firms are acquired or drift into obscurity. Once-powerful firms falter, restructure, revive, and falter again. Flawed strategic or organizational choices drive much of this failure, yet the root causes often appear to be subtler. What is it about the organization of professionals that

allows some firms to adapt to marketplace turmoil and prosper, while others lose share and gradually decline? Why do some firms seem to thrive on change while others melt down?

The answer, we believe, is found in the organization's culture. One reason we chose to study enduring "best-in-class" firms was to see whether cultural attributes contributed to their sustainability and prosperity. The evidence is clear: They do. Much as certain biological traits help species adapt more readily to evolutionary forces, certain cultural beliefs help firms adapt to economic turmoil and change.

Just as a firm's culture guides the decisions its members make, day by day, about the work they perform for clients and their relationships with colleagues, it shapes the ways that they respond to internal and external threats. If a firm's cultural beliefs are well developed along certain crucial dimensions, it is likely to overcome threats to its success and eventually prosper. If those beliefs are underdeveloped or seriously flawed, however, the firm is likely to fail.

While every organization's culture is distinctive and in many ways unique, outstanding firms are remarkably similar in the norms and beliefs that constitute their cultural core. Why the congruence? The explanation lies in the tensions that are an inherent part of every PSF's business model.

Tensions among partners who are both collegial and competitive, and who constantly vie for a pool of scarce human resources and for the rewards of their efforts. *Tensions within client teams*, which form and reform around specific assignments and provide a breeding ground for conflict at a personal level. Complex *tensions that cut through the entire organization*, as the community wrestles with issues across business lines, functional areas, and parts of the globe. *Tensions between the needs of stars and the demands of clients*, which can play out almost hour by hour. Finally, the perennial *tension between satisfying one generation of partners at the expense of coming generations*, between consuming today or investing for tomorrow.

The further we examined each of the firms in our study, the more evidence we found of the critical role that culture plays in containing these fundamental tensions. In every case, a core of beliefs had evolved within the firm, which helped its members accommodate the tensions endemic to their business. These beliefs did not link neatly to the tensions. It wasn't, and isn't, a matter of matching specific tensions with specific beliefs. Rather, each belief offset some or all of the tensions, more so or less so, depending on the circumstance at hand. These core beliefs guided the firm's behavior through business cycles and generations, exerting a powerful force for cohesion and ensuring their survival.

The Cultural Core

Whether we were looking at accounting firms or information technology companies, advertising agencies or law firms, five core beliefs characterized the way that the senior stars thought about their organization and their own relationship to it: belief in partnership, in extraordinary teams, in community, in stars first/clients first, and in perpetuity (see Figure A2).

Belief in Partnership

By "belief in partnership," we mean the conviction that senior stars are owners of the firm, and that regardless of the legal form of ownership, it must be governed as a partnership. As described in chapter 6, this means consensus building among the partners before major decisions about strategy are taken and the involvement of senior stars in other aspects of the governance of the firm, such as how compensation is allocated and who

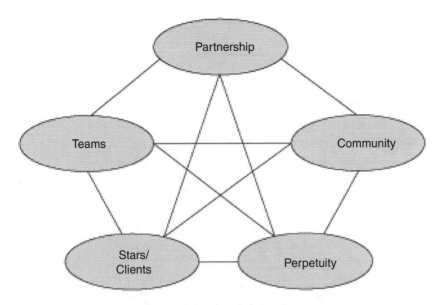

Figure A2 The Culture Core

is advanced into the ranks of the partnership. It also means that although it is all right for senior stars to compete with one another, it is *not* all right to let these rivalries get out of hand. The firm's success is the result of the efforts of the group as a whole. Respect for one another as colleagues is critical despite the fact that on an immediate, Monday-morning level, on any given day, one senior star may be pulling ahead of another in compensation, or in client portfolio size, or on another front altogether.

Diamond Cluster has been a public company since 1997. Nevertheless, the officers of the company still refer to, and think of one another as, "partners" and approve each other's compensation. If there were serious dissent about the compensation, the partners could remove the CEO and other senior managers. Similarly, the partners vote on new additions to their number. All of them feel that Diamond is their firm, and the leadership and management responsibility is spread among them, even though much of the equity is publicly owned. Mike Mikolajczyk, one of the firm's vice chairmen, explained their approach this way: "The partnership feeling is maintained through certain processes, like nomination. Every partner gets one vote, regardless of seniority or equity stake. So even the youngest junior partners feel like real partners and an important part of the process." An important corollary to these convictions, he noted, is the belief that "as owners, we are financially interdependent and must work hard for the firm's success."

A small event at Goldman Sachs, which took place at a leadership seminar in the early 1980s, says volumes about that firm's belief in partnership. A seminar for a group of Goldman Sachs partners was held just days after the firm had incurred a significant loss in its fixed-income trading activity. By coincidence, none of the partners from that part of the firm were in attendance. At the time, it was the custom to kick off these sessions with a talk and a question and answer session with the senior partner, John Weinberg. After some brief comments, the first question Weinberg was asked concerned the loss. Before he could answer, other partners expressed their concerns; implicit in their comments were criticisms of the fixed-income partners responsible for the loss.

Weinberg's response? If the firm was going to make as much money as it did on the upside, the partnership also had to expect some losses. He went on to confide that those involved had come to him personally—some of them practically in tears—and that nobody felt worse about what had happened than they did.

Implied in Weinberg's words—very thinly veiled—was the partnership mindset: Don't go around casting blame on your partners, who have already accepted their responsibility. The right thing to do is to support them. Just as you'll be supported if you encounter a rough patch.

Partnership, in the legal sense, was the founding form of many PSFs, and this belief takes its roots from that fact. The Goldman Sachs example we just mentioned took place long before the firm went public. But make no mistake; the partnership *mindset*—the core belief in a sense of shared destiny—is very real in all of these firms, regardless of ownership structure. The events described above, with a different cast of characters, could happen at Goldman today.

Belief in Extraordinary Teams

In all the firms we studied, the work of serving clients is performed by constantly changing teams of professionals. Because the need to serve clients well and in a timely fashion is paramount, life in those teams can be hectic and complicated. There's always a temptation for team members to want to look good and advance their own careers to the detriment of their teammates. This core belief discourages that kind of behavior. It also sends a strong signal about how you should relate to the people with whom you work every day on project teams: people with whom you may very well be competing for advancement or income, and under circumstances in which the tradeoffs between getting credit for yourself or for the team may be acute and personal.

This belief mitigates the tension among stars as they strive for personal success while simultaneously serving clients well together. (In that way, it is a natural extension of the belief in partnership that guides the seniormost stars of a firm.) Young stars learn that they must work together to succeed. Being an effective team member is what counts; that's how you succeed personally. In the words of Pat Gross, founder and chairman of the executive committee at American Management Systems:

> I think part of our advantage is the way we put effective teams together. If you deconstructed our teams and looked at the individuals, I'm not sure we could argue that the individuals by themselves are substantially better than other people. But there is a very strong, team-oriented culture at AMS. We say, "Let's get the right people together to solve a problem," and there's a lot of bonding that goes on. We have a common mission: the project team. It's the body of the company. When people come in, that's what they see. That's what they hear. When they come, they join a project team, and if they're not comfortable with that, they don't stay around very long. People try to communicate this in the recruiting process, because it's at the core of the way people at AMS think and operate.

Belief in Community

Belief in community is the proposition that at the end of the day we're all part of one firm, and we are expected to work together and help each other. A natural extension of the two beliefs that precede it, this one is all-encompassing and includes everyone, not just partners or senior stars, no matter the location. People in the United States, people overseas, people in every practice area (remember the example with which we started the chapter). This belief keeps everyone working together, regardless of specialty, level of experience, or geographic location. It keeps in check the tension that naturally develops as people identify with the goals of their particular part of the firm.

"People can't be worried about who gets the credit, and they can't be worried 'this is my deal, my client, stay out,"' said one Goldman Sachs banker, talking about the day-to-day efforts of the firm. "In order to serve clients, we need to bring together the skills related to hundreds of products and we have to bring to bear many parts of the firm. There needs to be a culture of excellent communication and commitment to the idea that if the firm does well, we will all do well, as opposed to 'I need to figure out how to look good, how I can do better.'"

As Patrick Pittard, CEO of Heidrick & Struggles, put it, "If you're in a ditch, you've got people who are there with you trying to get you out. You're not alone in troubled times. Say you have a search that has gone all the way through the process and you think you have it completed and then at the last minute the candidate bails out on you. Well, you send a voice mail and you get thirty responses on how to help yourself."

Belief in Stars First/Clients First

We've been arguing, up to this point, that the people you pay are more important than the people who pay you. We've been emphasizing that point because we recognize that the natural tendency is to put clients first, and we wanted to stress the strategic importance of stars. But the fact is, in these outstanding firms, stars and clients are considered equally important, and a natural and constant tension exists as each sector vies for the center position on the firm's radar. You can't have satisfied clients without stars, and you also can't have stars without satisfied clients.

The dilemma truly is that straightforward. If you're overinvesting in your clients, you'll lose your stars. But if you don't meet clients' needs because of your stars' desires, you won't be competitive. The belief that both are equally important enables firm managers to work for a balance in meeting conflicting demands between clients and stars. Diamond Cluster deals with the importance of both constituencies in an interesting way: Young professionals at Diamond are told "Clients first, firm second, yourself third." Partners, however, are told that the emphasis should be "Stars first, clients second, firm third." Whether stars or clients are given priority at any given time depends on circumstances. But over the long run, the balance between the two is critical to success. If the firm is to succeed, therefore, both these constituencies must be proactively managed, and each must think ultimately it occupies the number one spot.

Belief in Perpetuity

This core belief refers to the shared understanding, at the senior level, that you and your peers are building a firm that will transcend generations. That you're not only "in this together" with your current fellow partners, but also that part of your job is to help create a firm that will endure so future partners can succeed. It's the long view, and it drives people to behave selflessly in ways that support the firm.

Like many other New York law firms, Skadden Arps was challenged by the economic downturn in the late 1980s. The firm had always maintained a performance-based compensation scheme tied to each partner's contribution to firm results. But in the worsening economic climate, Joe Flom, one of the senior partners, along with several peers, became worried that the younger generation of partners would earn so little that the firm might lose many of them. Their proposed solution? That the older partners take a cut in pay so that the next generation could be better compensated. The partners approved the plan. And the result was not just a change in the partner compensation plan but also a reaffirmation that the firm was built to endure, that each generation should worry about the next.

What happens when questions arise about how to distribute the wealth among different generations at your firm? How do clients get passed on from retiring partners to their younger peers? This belief in perpetuity guides those kinds of events—balancing the tensions between older and younger stars and achieving results that work for the long-term success of the firm.

Culture and Consequences

In aggregate, these core beliefs constitute a way of thinking about how an individual star fits into the ecosystem of a firm. The beliefs shape how people behave on Monday morning, but they do not *specify* that behavior in an absolute sense. The belief in partnership, for example, motivates senior stars to collaborate as partners; the details of that collaboration change as the partnership expands and diversifies. Just as a belief in *democracy* or *capitalism* propels governments and markets, so do core beliefs propel outstanding PSFs.

The interdependence of these core beliefs is striking. In the absence of one or more beliefs, a firm will eventually stumble. Without "partnership," a firm will gradually disintegrate at the top, as senior stars compete among themselves. Without "extraordinary teams," clients will be underserved and promising young stars will resign for more fulfilling employment opportunities. Without "community," an organization of independent silos will rapidly evolve—a place where knowledge is hoarded, resources are never shared, and quality inevitably deteriorates. If a culture is unable to balance stars and clients, sooner or later one will win at the expense of the other (and either stars or clients will defect). Finally, without a belief in perpetuity, a firm will, at a minimum, *underinvest* in the future—and more than likely sell out to the highest bidder whenever an attractive cash-out opportunity presents itself—without considering whether this is in the long-term interest of the firm's owners.

There is no escaping the direct linkage between culture and consequences. In robust economic times, commercial success may mask cultural deterioration. In downturns, the flaws become readily apparent. As the Japanese say, "A falling tide exposes all rocks." Culturally strong firms accommodate and adapt to recessions, while culturally flawed firms struggle to hold ground. Culture can emerge as the defining competitive advantage, in part because it is impossible to copy. Individuals in great firms rally around a powerful cultural core, while in other firms, they obsess over their personal circumstances as their business flounders.

Consider Goldman Sachs, whose business principles reflect the firm's commitment to its core beliefs. Written down many years ago by John Whitehead, then one of the managing partners, they are still published in the annual report each year (see Box A1). The message is clear to employees and to clients. Regular publication is one small way that Goldman nurtures commitment to these core beliefs.

Culture Binds

Goldman Sachs's decision to go public might provide the best example of a case where culture—including the firm's core beliefs—sustained the firm through a time of incredible change.

For over ten years, under the leadership of three capable individuals, Steve Friedman, Jon Corzine, and Hank Paulson, the partners of Goldman Sachs debated the merits of selling some of the firm's equity into the public market. The partners had decided to take on two limited partners, the Bishop Estate and Sumitomo Bank, to raise needed capital in 1986, 1992, and 1994 without abandoning the partnership form of ownership. But the

Box A1 Goldman Sachs's Business Principles

1. Our clients' interests always come first. Our experience shows that if we serve our clients well, our own success will follow.
2. Our assets are our people, capital, and reputation. If any of these is ever diminished, the last is the most difficult to restore. We are dedicated to complying fully with the letter and spirit of the laws, rules, and ethical principles that govern us. Our continued success depends upon unswerving adherence to this standard.
3. We take great pride in the professional quality of our work. We have an uncompromising determination to achieve excellence in everything we undertake. Though we may be involved in a wide variety and heavy volume of activity, we would, if it came to a choice, rather be best than biggest.
4. We stress creativity and imagination in everything we do. While recognizing that the old way may still be the best way, we constantly strive to find a better solution to a client's problems. We pride ourselves on having pioneered many of the practices and techniques that have become standard in the industry.
5. We make an unusual effort to identify and recruit the very best person for every job. Although our activities are measured in billions of dollars, we select our people one by one. In a service business, we know that without the best people, we cannot be the best firm.
6. We offer our people the opportunity to move ahead more rapidly than is possible at most other places. We have yet to find the limits to the responsibility that our best people are able to assume. Advancement depends solely on ability, performance, and contribution to the firm's success, without regard to race, color, religion, sex, age, national origin, disability, sexual orientation, or any other impermissible criterion of circumstances.
7. We stress teamwork in everything we do. While individual creativity is always encouraged, we have found that team effort often produces the best results. We have no room for those who put their personal interests ahead of the interests of the firm and its clients.
8. The dedication of our people to the firm and the intense effort they give their jobs are greater than one finds in most other organizations. We think that this is an important part of our success.
9. Our profits are a key to our success. They replenish our capital and attract and keep our best people. It is our practice to share our profits generously with all who helped create them. Profitability is crucial to our future.
10. We consider our size an asset that we try to preserve. We want to be big enough to undertake the largest project that any of our clients could contemplate, yet small enough to maintain the loyalty, the intimacy, and the esprit de corps that we will treasure and that contribute greatly to our success.

11. We constantly strive to anticipate the rapidly changing needs of our clients and to develop new services to meet those needs. We know that the world of finance will not stand still and that complacency can lead to extinction.

12. We regularly receive confidential information as part of our normal client relationships. To breach a confidence or to use confidential information improperly or carelessly would be unthinkable.

13. Our business is highly competitive, and we aggressively seek to expand our client relationships. However, we must always be fair competitors and must never denigrate other firms.

14. Integrity and honesty are at the heart of our business. We expect our people to maintain high ethical standards in everything they do, both in their work for the firm and in their personal lives.

Source: © Goldman Sachs. Reprinted with permission.

discussions about becoming a corporation and selling equity to the public continued throughout the 1990s. At least six times, the partners vetted the issues thoroughly, declining to go public for the last time in 1996.

In 1998, the discussions again gained momentum, culminating with a Quaker-style meeting of all 190 partners at a location outside New York City at which the partners aired their hopes and concerns about the proposed public offering. "For people who have devoted their lives to this place, it was exhausting, but in some ways amazing," one partner told the *New York Times*. "People did not hold back."

The arguments for selling 15 percent of the firm's equity to the public were mainly financial. It was a means to realize the immense value of the firm's equity for its partners and to raise capital for the firm's future.

Most apropos to the topic of culture were the reasons put forth for not going public. The fear was that the core belief in the partnership, as we have called it, would be lost, endangering the firm's ability to serve clients and attract stars. At the final meeting, partner after partner, even those in favor of the idea, voiced this concern.

Finally the partners voted for the IPO, in essence authorizing the firm's management committee to work out the offering terms and timing.

The IPO isn't the end of the tale, however. The firm sold 15 percent of its equity to the public (and subsequently made a secondary offering of 40 million shares) and Goldman Sachs is legally a corporation, but the senior leaders and the partners have done all they can to retain a partnership culture. The firm retains the partner compensation plan for which up-and-coming stars are chosen, just as before they were elected into the partnership. The firm retains a partnership committee as one way of giving voice to its partners. Meetings of the partners are still held to discuss important issues and decisions. In the eyes of the public and the capital markets, Goldman Sachs may be a legal corporation, but in the eyes of its senior stars it is culturally still a partnership, and they are working to sustain this culture.

Convictions, which people hold dear, are not easy to alter. So when a decision that might affect "the way we do things" comes to bear, it's only natural that a partnership—and an organization at large—would be reluctant to make the move. Recognizing that a strong culture is like glue can help you overcome such concerns. Culture binds organization, strategy, and stars together in the face of significant requirements for change. It can help retain core beliefs and values while allowing major changes in strategy or organization.

So when a firm goes from private to public, as Goldman Sachs, Korn/Ferry, and so many others have done, the firm's leaders can use the cultural beliefs associated with the partnership to maintain the alignment that would otherwise be threatened. The formal trappings associated with public shareholders—quarterly earnings reports, a board of directors, for example—can be handled in a manner that supports rather than threatens beliefs about partnership and community.

The same holds true for international expansion where a firm's culture can provide a blueprint for foreign offices. As McKinsey expanded globally to eighty offices in thirty-two countries, replicating the culture was a critical imperative. Despite immense variations in nationalities and time zones, professionals share a common set of beliefs about partnership, teams, community, and clients and stars.

Culture is a stronger force for unity and coherence than any formal document could ever be because the stars of a firm with a strong culture have an emotional commitment to their beliefs. The Goldmans and McKinseys of the world have been able to maintain consistent strategic and organizational approaches due to the strength of their cultures. Wherever these firms operate—from New York to London to Delhi to Tokyo—their professionals share a culture that binds them into common practices, sustains their alignment, and gives them an advantage in attracting clients. Clients perceive a clear and consistent strategic identity because the firm's professionals—wherever they work—share a set of beliefs that maintain this consistency.

This is especially true when firms are experiencing rapid growth. Growth delivers a double whammy; it exacerbates organizational complexity and introduces legions of "culturally raw" recruits. Both characteristics may easily undermine or confuse cultural beliefs. When a firm hires partners from industry or completes an acquisition, the dynamics are even more challenging. Yet firms with strong cultural beliefs are bound together despite these centrifugal forces. Weaker cultures on the other hand are blown asunder. This in part explains why mergers and acquisitions of PSFs so often fail in retaining stars. The culture of the acquirer overwhelms the culture of the acquired, and this alienates the stars of the acquired firm, causing them to leave.

Strong cultures bind together organizations during times of strategic change—ranging from IPOs to international expansion to acquisitions. Once again, core cultural beliefs help sustain competitive advantage for established firms. How might this apply to first-generation PSFs?

Culture Builds

First-generation professional firms always struggle and most do not succeed; building an enduring firm is exceptionally challenging. Nowhere was this more evident than in Internet-focused technology consulting, a sector that experienced a spectacular run-up and an equally spectacular fall. Although few of these companies will survive, much can be learned from the role that culture played in their rapid growth and subsequent collapse.

In 1996, Bob Gett, founder and CEO of newly formed Viant, began to create his organization's culture from scratch. After a lengthy professional career, at firms ranging from Fidelity Software Development Company to Cambridge Technology Partners, he well understood the importance of culture. In fact, to emphasize the power of culture, he dubbed himself the "Chief Cultural Officer." While Viant's culture was a critical ingredient in its ramp up to over $150 million revenue in four years, it was even more important as the industry collapsed and Viant saw its market capitalization decline by 95 percent.

Viant's belief in partnership was forged as Gett recruited his senior team. Strong capabilities were necessary but not sufficient to get in on the ground floor of this "new economy" consulting firm. "I looked for culture builders who shared a dream about Viant's potential," explained Gett. These values and beliefs became the common denominator across what was otherwise a diverse leadership team.

The top ten leaders (they were never referred to as "managers" or "executives") met for a day to write down their shared beliefs as a touch-stone for the expanding organization. Even before they specified the full details of their business plan, these "partners" shook hands on their cultural contract. Their desks were arranged together in the large open space that was the firm's new office. "We were desk to desk every day," said Gett. "There was no escaping our shared beliefs as leaders in this venture."

The cultural belief in extraordinary teams was integral to Viant's competi-tive strategy. Traditionally, clients had purchased business strategy services, creative services, and technology assistance from different firms. Viant intended to change this paradigm, to blend the three disciplines from very different worlds, to innovate at the seams where the three intersect. To better serve clients, Viant needed to somehow operationally integrate the strategic skills of a Bain & Company with Ogilvy & Mather's creative talent and IBM Consulting's technology capabilities—and to do this effectively on every single client team!

Part of the solution resided in performance management. Teams (rather than individuals) were held jointly accountable for projects. Consistent salary ranges and performance criteria were applied regardless of a consul-tant's expertise. Peer review became an integral component of annual performance reviews, which subsequently determined bonuses and career progression.

Performance management systems reinforced the cultural belief in di-verse but integrated teams. As the firm grew, the culture shaped and informed behavior, encouraging opinionated consultants to be compas-sionate about each other's views. The belief in extraordinary teams (and a potential competitive advantage) was born.

Viant's core beliefs in partnership and teams provided the foundation for a pervasive belief in community. This was not some "feel good" factor to add a dose of "cool" to the business mix. On the contrary, this cultural dimension was carefully designed to help deliver on the company's strategic ambitions.

"People here are really pounding away," explained Gett during the firm's heyday. "They have to feel great about sitting next to other guys and gals in the room." Thus the rationale for an office layout that contributed to spontaneous interactions. "Vianteers," as Gett called them, also abhorred hierarchy. It took four years before the community generated its first organizational chart.

Office size was capped at 125 people to avoid diluting the sense of community. New offices were "spawned" by permanent and temporary transfers to new locations where their primary job was to inoculate the emerging communities with Viant's cultural beliefs.

A belief in community was not only critical to retain and motivate stars in an exceptionally competitive space; it was absolutely necessary to facilitate effective knowledge sharing. Gett believed that typical consulting firms deliver client value that rests primarily on the strength of an individual team, rather than on the knowledge and energy of an entire firm. Gett intended to harness the "power of the community" to develop a culture of knowledge sharing and learning, a place where "silos" and consulting "rock stars" gave way to selfless collaboration. In 2000, *Fortune* profiled Viant in an article entitled "The House That Knowledge Built."2 It referenced community-building tactics ranging from a three-week new-employee orientation (called "Quick Start"), to staffing rotations that created networks of personal relationships across the firm. While these systems reinforced a sense of community, it was the cultural belief that dictated daily knowledge sharing across organizational boundaries.

The community orientation was deliberately designed to provide excellence in servicing clients. How, then, did such a client-centered culture trade off between its star performers and its important clients? As Gett explained: "We always take the high road in balancing the demands of our clients against the needs of our consultants, even though we may suffer short-term pain as a consequence. The high road means that we never compromise the client situation, that we primarily take their view. Our cultural belief is that people will be taken care of, that their sacrifices will be recognized."

Trading off in favor of current clients did not mean sacrificing the future of the firm, however. In a powerful cultural statement, Viant management decided to constrain their growth during the 1998/1999 halcyon days of market expansion. "We were concerned that excessive growth would undermine our culture and potentially create client excellence problems," said Gett. Despite competitive pressures to maximize growth, spiced by media commentary that Viant was falling behind, Viant held growth to a modest 100 percent per year (compared to the 300 to 400 percent typical for the industry at the time). "We wanted a culture centered on being the best, not the biggest, to strive for mind share rather than market share," Gett proclaimed.

This perspective and the values it reveals were central to Gett's dream of Viant's endurance. "Viant was not 'built to flip' like so many venture capital–funded start-ups," he told us. "I have always been driven by commitment to people and excellence, rather than ego or money. Hopefully, Viant will be 'built to last.'"

At this time, the jury is still out on his ambition. The bursting bubble of e-commerce has led to profit shortfalls, layoffs, and consolidation throughout Viant's industry. Once again, however, Viant's cultural beliefs have come to its aid—though probably not enough to save it. Because the firm nurtured a belief in perpetuity early on, employees were better able to view the market turmoil from a long-term perspective. The intense pain of layoffs was tempered by the understanding that it was "the right thing to do for the firm." "Survivors" were motivated to fight the good fight and do whatever it took to survive and prosper. Voluntary turnover has remained at a low (by industry standards) 12 percent despite the harsh reality that employee equity is virtually destroyed.

Whatever the future holds in store for Viant, the value created by its culture is unmistakeable.

Culture Bends

A strong culture is a common attribute of successful professional firms. Most of the leaders of the outstanding firms we've interviewed, in fact, believe that culture is one of their key competitive advantages. McKinsey's legendary leader, Marvin Bower, for example, consistently emphasized the importance of being a "true professional" regardless of circumstance. That cultural attribute is still central to the firm because it is a large part of what makes McKinsey, McKinsey. It is a critical piece of the firm's strategic identity and a strong draw for clients.

But if culture can be a competitive advantage, it can also be a competitive disadvantage. What if a fast-paced, aggressively informal e-commerce consultancy is pitching to a traditional, conservative, industrial company? What if that consulting firm—whose livelihood depends on a client base that includes such traditional companies—is unable to present its case in a way that resonates with the manufacturer's executives? If your culture is working against the firm, you have to change it. You start from where you are—what lies ahead is up to you.

Consider how dramatically the culture at Ogilvy & Mather changed under the leadership of Charlotte Beers. When Beers took over as CEO and chairman of Ogilvy & Mather Worldwide in 1992, the firm was losing important clients and facing declining revenues. The agency had just been acquired in a hostile takeover by British holding company WPP, and morale was low. Star performers knew that their game plan wasn't working, but they were suspicious of Beers, of Sir Martin Sorrel, WPP's CEO, who had chosen her, and of change under Beers's rule. Sorrel, they feared, was focused only on the bottom line, and wasn't interested in preserving the dedication to creative values in which they deeply believed—values instilled by the firm's legendary founder David Ogilvy. Beers, for her part, was also personally suspect because, as she put it, she was "the daughter of a Texas cowboy," whose past success had not been with a big international Madison Avenue agency, but rather with a smaller, domestic firm in Chicago.

Put another way, the stars at Ogilvy were worried that Sorrel and Beers represented great threats to the firm's founding culture—a culture they were proud of and part of—a culture that had once made the firm a great success.

Beers understood that, and what she did showed the firm's stars that not only did she acknowledge and respect Ogilvy's culture of creativity but she also knew what to do to build on that foundation, instill new, critical core beliefs, and return the firm to greatness in its new context.

In her first few months at Ogilvy, Beers spent a lot of time talking with investors and clients. She knew that the culture at Ogilvy was something to be preserved and strengthened, but she also came to the realization that the firm had no clear direction. By May 1992, she had mustered a group of Ogilvy employees—some heads of key offices or regions, some creatives, some account directors—who she felt were on her wavelength. These were people who wanted to sustain the culture but also understood the need to reinvent the agency's focus and structure. This "thirsty for change" group, as it was called, met first in May 1992 in Vienna, essentially to raise issues, to talk about what it would take to reinvent and revitalize the firm. Among their primary concerns was Ogilvy's geographic fragmentation—the firm was run essentially as a group of national kingdoms and was not set up to meet the increasing global needs of multinational clients in a seamless way. Basically, the firm's culture lacked a core belief in community.

They met next in August 1992 at the English resort Chewton Glen. Out of that meeting came the "Chewton Glen Declaration," which set three strategic goals for 1993: (1) client security—focusing energy on current clients; (2) Better Work, More Often—a call to move beyond the traditional Ogilvy credo, "We Sell, Or Else," and develop ways to make brand the binding focus of the firm; and (3) Financial Discipline—a call to get control over the firm's resources. Mostly, the goals were a call to reinforce the firm's values about creativity, but in a way that better met client needs.

Shortly thereafter, Beers made a major change in the firm's structure. She created a third dimension in its matrix organization: Worldwide Client Service. (The other two are geographic and functional.) The purpose of the new dimension was to put a capable leader, Kelly O'Dea, in charge of encouraging cooperation and coordination in serving global clients across the high national barriers that were part of the old culture. When the agency won the IBM worldwide account, the need for the change became evident to everyone in the firm; without the new structure—and the corresponding new belief in the "global community" philosophy—Ogilvy could never have provided seamless service to such a multinational client.

Reduced to its essentials, the old culture just didn't work as well as it needed to in a changing marketplace. Beers and her "thirsty for change" friends used their leadership skills, their new ideas about the importance of brand, and their new structure to support the important embedded beliefs about creativity and tie them more closely to the brand needs of clients. At the same time, they enhanced the core belief about the importance of community.

So What?

Each generation transmits its culture to the next. In older firms, that means that the culture has been passed through many generations, often through stories—some accurate, others probably myths. What matters isn't absolute veracity but rather that the intended message gets through.

Remember the partners at Goldman Sachs, for example, who say they received their first performance review from former senior partner Gus Levy while they were in the men's room with him. True? Well. . . . But even if the accounts aren't entirely accurate, they're amusing, they get attention, and the message is clear: "We believe in performance reviews and they're going to be direct and personal."

Figures like Goldman Sachs's Levy, McKinsey's Bower, Ogilvy & Mather's David Ogilvy, and Fulbright & Jaworski's Leon Jaworski become somewhat larger than life through such oral histories. But beware. It's too easy to think of culture as something personal—the stuff of legends and heroes. In fact, the notion that culture flows from any few leaders—no matter what their stature—is true mostly in a figurative sense. No single leader can embody the culture of any given firm, especially if that firm has hundreds, or thousands, or tens of thousands of employees. Most of the members of the firm never see the top brass. And if they do, it's for a few minutes each year, when they are on a stage or appearing in a videotape.

A firm's culture will be influenced to a modest extent by the sheer force of personality coming from the person on that stage. What they say and how they say it does have an impact. But, as we've said, culture is influenced more substantively through the decisions that a person—and "partners" throughout the firm—make, which then shape behaviors, which subsequently become part of "how things are done here."

In other words, if you're the leader of your firm, you may be the walking personification of the culture you inherited when you took office. And that may be a good thing. But your firm's culture isn't set in stone. It isn't ever "done." The way that you will affect it most is through the strategic and organizational choices you make or facilitate every Monday morning.

From My Workspace to Yours, Online

"Innovation, Communication, and a New Definition of 'Friend from Work'"

An Interview with Constantine von Hoffman, Senior Editor, *Brandweek Magazine*, Author, Collateral Damage blog: www.collateraldamage.biz

Q: YouTube, MySpace, Blogs, Plogs—how have all of these changed the way we work?

A: Way back in the time, like before 1995, it used to be that the best informed people in the world were the journalists who had access to what were called news wires—feeds from news gathering services like Associated Press and Reuters. They would see stories that were going on all around the world that never made it into the paper or onto a newscast. Now, because of the web in general and blogs and blog aggregators in particular, anyone can have that. I have a huge list of blogs that I keep an eye on through Bloglines and I can scan them rapidly looking for the stuff that interests me without having to read every little thing or dig up the information myself. In essence, I have a lot of experts out there doing research for me, digging up stories and facts that I would never find on my own. I actually don't use MySpace because I have never found it useful for getting information, although a lot of other reporters frequently finds trends and ideas there.

Q: But what's the "net, net" of that new ability? Do you think people are:

a) Spending more time at the computer, but the time is really useful because people are learning things that are making them more productive?

b) Spending more time at the computer but in large part not learning anything that significantly affects their work?

c) Spending more time at the computer, learning more interesting and useful things, but losing, at the same time, a piece of the interpersonal dynamic at work that people used to call "synergy"—and that executives seemed very fond of touting as an "intangible strength" in corporate life?

Or is it another scenario entirely?

A: Are people more productive because of the net? Yep. For me, that takes the shape of spending less time chasing down little stuff when I could be focusing on big stuff. Finding out basic info about a company, like earnings, HQ location, phone numbers, as opposed to talking to people about whatever story I'm researching.

Are people spending more time at the computer but in large part not learning anything that significantly affects their work? Maybe. I don't think the web has made us any smarter as individuals. There is now a higher likelihood that you will be exposed to information that you would not otherwise have had. Once that is done, it's still all in the thinking and the application. Einstein didn't have a computer. Matt Drudge does. Who knows how much more (if anything) Einstein could have done with the access to info that we have now. Drudge just regurgitates rumors or—if you're feeling kind—highlights other people's work but, thanks to the net thing, he has a huge audience and moments of huge influence. And no original thinking whatsoever. That said, connectors are important. We need people who watch a lot of places and point things out that the rest of us would miss.

Are people spending more time at their computers and less with actual human beings in the company? Yes. My wife is much closer to people who work with her online on projects than she is with people in her office who don't work on projects with her. Has this helped or hurt corporate synergies? Too soon to tell. Companies have always had problems keeping people connected and informed. The web hasn't made those problems go away and it has given them another excuse to hide behind: Instead of just sending out newsletters, they now run blogs and websites and send e-mails that everyone discards just like the old newsletters. It is still up to individual managers and workers to make sure they connect.

In short, people are still, by and large, stupid. The web-eroni makes it easier to connect with other people who share your interests, but that's not always the person in the next cubicle. Is that a plus for business . . . I don't know.

Or, as someone else put it, you keep giving them books and giving them books and they keep chewing on the covers.

Q: What about the effect (possible) of blogs, plogs, etc. on innovation? A *Wall Street Journal* story (Thursday, October 5, 2006, page B1, "How Demon Wife Became a Media Star and Other Tales of the 'Blook'" in Japan" by Yukari Iwatani Kane, said:

> Six years ago, a Japanese businessman went online to vent about his domineering wife. Blogging daily under the pen name "Kazuma," he detailed how she grabbed food from is plate, sent him shopping in a typhoon, and made him sleep in the living room when he caught a cold. Now his terrifying spouse is famous as Oniyome, or "demon wife," the star of a book, a television drama, a comic-book serialization, a videogame and coming soon, a movie. *Demon Wife Diaries*, as the book and its spin-offs are titled, is at the forefront of a trend in new media emerging in Japan—blogs, chat rooms, and other Internet formats are increasingly providing

the inspiration, and in many cases, the verbatim content, for books, television shows, and other old-media products.

What is your take on that?

A: Blooks are a growing phenomenon—someone even gives out awards for blooks. The first one I was aware of that made a big splash was by someone under the pen name Salaam Pax, who blogged from Iraq during our invasion and his posts were later turned into a blook. A couple of U.S. military veterans of the George W. Bush Desert Classic have also had some small success with blooks but nothing like what happened in Japan, which is probably sui generis. Several other writers have tried to spin their success as bloggers into books but without much real impact. The biggest of these that I can think of are Wonkette and Washingtonienne. Both are D.C.-based and focused blogs. The former combined a fun attitude and light sexual repartee to shine a gossipy but not all that tawdry light on D.C. (Great quote from Anna Marie Cox who was Wonkette: "I wanted to ruin someone's day, not their life.") The other one was a blog about the sexual adventures of a comely female capital hill staffer. Both then wrote novels, which went approximately nowhere.

Blogs don't make good books because they are an immediate reaction to the events of the day. They are all about the topical and short-term. Because of that they usually focus on things that have disappeared from someone's memory a month later. They don't have the depth to support a full book and if they do they're not being true blogs. A blog is your note book, except usually with less detail. It's the perfect format for the ADD generation.

That said, blogs, chat rooms and other Internet formats are increasingly providing the inspiration, and in many cases, the verbatim content, for books, television shows, and other old-media products. Yeah, the old media is going to continue to chase the new. We haven't seen the widespread use of it that Japan has but Japan has a monocultural society where we definitely do not.

Q: Could you comment on the potential upsides and downsides of web marketing. Is it getting easier to create a brand? Protect a brand?

A: The web has fundamentally changed how companies have to think of what a brand is. It used to be that marketers thought that their brand was whatever they told customers it was. Marketers operated under the illusion that they were in control of the brand. This was because communication methods all worked in one direction—TV, print or whatever—were all about telling people a message and had no way for the people to respond. This illusion allowed marketers to ignore the communication that went on between consumers.

The reality though is that how people talk to each other about a brand has always been what really defined a brand. Now thanks to the Web a lot more people are having a lot more conversations about brands. Pretty much every brand now has an unofficial site where its fans/consumers gather to swap rumors and talk about their experience with the product. This runs the gamut from expensive cars to video games to things like WD40 where people swap tips on new uses for the stuff. Any marketer who doesn't at least regularly check out these sites is an idiot. The smart marketers use them as a place to have actual conversations with their consumers. The tough part for marketers is that now it really is a conversation. If you just listen and don't react then you will get a richly deserved rep as brand that doesn't care about its consumers. You don't have to do whatever it is that these people suggest but you do have to give them straight honest answers to their concerns.

Brands are just as hard to create and protect as they were before. The brand has always relied first and foremost on the product or service it delivers to establish its value. What's tougher now is that if a product or service screws up everyone knows about it very quickly. Fortunately, the same is true when customers are happy with a product or service.

Q: There's an article in the *Wall Street Journal* (Thursday, March 22, 2007) entitled "A New Force in Advertising—Protest by E-mail" (by Christina Passariello in Paris, Keith Johnson in Madrid and Suzanne Vranica in New York). The article talks about how e-mail protests caused Dolce & Gabbana to pull an image in reaction to strong protests, many sent via e-mail.

A: This is another example of the change in what it means to market a brand. Letter campaigns have always been around and sometimes gained enough momentum to catch the eye of the media. Where this used to take a while to get organized and reach critical mass, today it can happen over night. It also can involve a lot of people who never would have known about it before. In the D&G story, a lot of web sites were able to post the ads and people who never picked up a fashion magazine saw them. This hurt the company's rep with the general public—most importantly with investors. It's impossible to contain stories now. While there's no doubt that D&G wanted to be provocative, if they'd listened better and first showed the ad to people who didn't work for them or their ad agency then they would have been able to see the problem before it happened.

Q: One last question, returning us to the topic of culture at work. What parts of the workforce do you think stand to "gain" the most from these increasingly popular—and emerging—forms of communication? Where is this all taking us, in the context of the way we work?

A: The optimistic take would be that everyone will gain as we become more able to swap stories with people working on similar projects in far away places. People will be able to see what other people are doing that does and doesn't work. Less time will be spent re-inventing the wheel.

The pessimistic take is that it will narrow who we talk to. We'll only follow those issues and projects that we are already interested in. People may have greater knowledge of their specialty but less knowledge about bigger issues or what is going on elsewhere. Cross-fertilization, which has always been hard for companies, will be even harder.

Reality will probably be somewhere in between. The biggest risk for companies is thinking that technology will take the place of good management. Chat rooms, e-mail, wikis, blogs and the like are better tools than companies have ever had before. But tools do not use themselves.

Bibliography

The list below represents a variety of books and other materials that include references to, and discussions of, business and organizational culture. This list is not intended to be comprehensive, but to showcase the breadth of resources available on the subject of business culture.

Angel, Karen. *Inside Yahoo! Reinvention and the Road Ahead*. Hoboken, NJ: Wiley, 2002.

Battelle, John. *The Search: How Google and Its Rivals Rewrote the Rules of Business and Transformed Our Culture*. New York: Portfolio, 2005.

Brands, H. W. *Masters of Enterprise: Giants of American Business from John Jacob Astor and J.P. Morgan to Bill Gates and Oprah Winfrey*. New York: Free Press, 1999.

Buffett, Warren E. *The Essays of Warren Buffett: Lessons for Corporate America*. The Cunningham Group, 2001.

Carnegie, Andrew. *The Empire of Business*. New York: Doubleday, Doran & Co., 1902 (reprinted by Kessinger Publishing, 2004).

Cohen, Adam. *The Perfect Store: Inside eBay*. New York: Little, Brown, 2002.

Cohen, Ben, and Jerry Greenfield. *Ben & Jerry's Double Dip: How to Run a Values Led Business and Make Money Too*. New York: Simon & Schuster, 1998 (paperback reprint).

Daisey, Mike. *21 Dog Years: A Cube Dweller's Tale*. The Free Press, Simon & Schuster, 2003 (Trade Paperback Edition).

Dell, Michael, with Catherine Fredman. *Direct from Dell: Strategies that Revolutionized an Industry.* New York: Collins, 2000 (paperback reprint).

Deutschman, Alan. *The Second Coming of Steve Jobs.* New York: Broadway, 2001 (paperback reprint).

Drucker, Peter. *The Essential Drucker: The Best of Sixty Years of Peter Drucker's Essential Writings on Management.* New York: Collins, 2003 (Paperback).

Ellison, Nicole B. *Telework and Social Change: How Technology is Reshaping the Boundaries between Home and Work.* Westport, CT: Praeger Publishers, 2004.

Forbes Magazine Staff. *Forbes Greatest Business Stories of All Time.* Hoboken, NJ: Wiley, 1997.

Frieberg, Kevin, and Jackie Freiberg. *Nuts! Southwest Airlines' Crazy Recipe for Business and Personal Success.* New York: Broadway, 1998 (paperback reprint).

Galford, Robert, and Anne Seibold Drapeau. *The Trusted Leader: Bringing Out the Best in Your People and Your Company.* New York: The Free Press, 2002.

Galford, Robert, and Regina Maruca. *Your Leadership Legacy: Why Looking Toward the Future Will Make You a Better Leader Today.* Boston: Harvard Business School Press, 2006.

Gates, Bill. *Business @ the Speed of Thought: Succeeding in the Digital Economy.* New York: Warner, 2000 (paperback reprint).

Gerstner, Louis V., Jr. *Who Says Elephants Can't Dance? Inside IBM's Historic Turnaround.* New York: Collins, 2002.

Gilley, Jerry W., and Ann Gilley. *The Manager as Coach.* Westport, CT: Praeger Publishers, 2007.

Gittell, Jody Hoffer. *The Southwest Airlines Way: Using the Power of Relationships to Achieve High Performance.* New York: McGraw-Hill, 2002.

Goldman, Robert, and Stephen Papson. *Nike Culture: The Sign of the Swoosh.* Thousand Oaks, CA: Sage Publications, 1999.

Grove, Andrew S. *Only the Paranoid Survive: How to Achieve a Success That's Just a Disaster Away.* New York: Currency, 1999 (paperback reprint).

Haasen, Adolf, and Gordon F. Shea. *New Corporate Cultures that Motivate.* Westport, CT: Praeger Publishers, 2003.

Hill, Sam. *Sixty Trends in Sixty Minutes.* Hoboken, NJ: John Wiley & Sons, Inc., 2002 (A Brandweek Book).

Jackson, Tim. *Inside Intel: Andy Grove and the Rise of the World's Most Powerful Chip Company.* New York: Plume, 1998 (paperback reprint).

Kamprad, Ingvar, and Bertil Torekull. *Leading by Design: The IKEA Story*. New York: Collins, 1999.

Koehn, Nancy F. *Brand New: How Entrepreneurs Earned Consumers' Trust from Wedgwood to Dell*. Boston: Harvard Business School Press, 2001.

Lawler, Edward E., III, and James O'Toole. *America at Work: Choices and Challenges*, New York: Palgrave MacMillan, 2006.

Lawler, Edward E., III, and Christopher G. Worley. *Built to Change: How to Achieve Sustained Organizational Effectiveness*. San Francisco: Jossey-Bass (A Wiley Imprint), 2006.

Lipton, Mark. *Guiding Growth: How Vision Keeps Companies on Course*. Boston, Harvard Business School Press, 2003.

Magretta, Joan (with the collaboration of Nan Stone). *What Management Is: How it Works and Why It Is Everyone's Business*. Boston: Free Press, 2002.

Martin, Joanne. *Organizational Culture: Mapping the Terrain* (Foundations for Organizational Science Series). Thousand Oaks, CA: Sage Publications, 2001.

Maruca, Regina Fazio, ed. *What Managers Say/What Employees Hear: Connecting with Your Front Line (So They'll Connect with Customers)*. Westport, CT: Praeger Publishers, 2006.

Mayo, Anthony J., Nitin Nohria, and Laura G. Singleton. *Paths to Power: How Insiders and Outsiders Shaped American Business Leadership*. Boston: Harvard Business School Press, 2006.

McLean, Bethany, and Peter Elkind. *The Smartest Guys in the Room: The Amazing Rise and Scandalous Fall of Enron*. New York: Portfolio, 2003.

Movers and Shakers: The 100 Most Influential Figures in Modern Business. New York: Basic Books, 2003.

Neff, Thomas J., and James Citrin. *Lessons from the Top: The 50 Most Successful Business Leaders in America—and What You Can Learn From Them*. New York: Currency, 2001.

O'Neil, William J. *Business Leaders and Success: 55 Top Business Leaders and How They Achieved Greatness*. New York: McGraw-Hill, 2003.

Pauchant, Thierry C. *Ethics and Spirituality at Work*. Westport, CT: Quorum Books, 2002.

Perseus Publishing Staff. *Business: The Ultimate Resource*. Cambridge, MA: Perseus Publishing, 2002.

Roddick, Anita. *Take It Personally: How to Make Conscious Choices to Change the World*. San Francisco: Red Wheel/Weiser, 2001.

Rothman, Howard. *Companies That Changed the World: Incisive Profiles of the 50*

Organizations—Large & Small—That Have Shaped the Course of Modern Business. Franklin Lakes, NJ: Career Press, 2001.

Sandberg, Jared. Columnist for the *Wall Street Journal*. Writes a regular column entitled "Cubicle Culture," which is reprinted on a variety of websites, including the *Wall Street Journal* website, www.careerjournal.com (executive career site of the *Wall Street Journal* online) and also www.postgazette.com.

Schein, Edgar. *Organizational Culture and Leadership* (The Jossey-Bass Business & Management Series). San Francisco: Jossey-Bass (A Wiley Imprint), 2004.

Schultz, Howard. *Pour Your Heart into It: How Starbucks Built a Company One Cup at a Time*. New York: Hyperion, 1999 (paperback reprint).

Slater, Robert. *Jack Welch & the GE Way: Management Insights & Leadership Secrets of the Legendary CEO*. New York: McGraw-Hill, 1998.

Slater, Robert. *The Wal-Mart Triumph: Inside the World's #1 Company*. New York: Portfolio, 2004 (paperback reprint).

Sloan, Alfred P., Jr. *My Years with General Motors*. New York: Currency, 1990 reissue (originally published, 1964).

Swisher, Kara. *There Must Be a Pony in Here Somewhere: The AOL Time Warner Debacle and the Quest for the Digital Future*. New York: Three Rivers, 2004 (paperback reprint).

Tedlow, Richard S. *Giants of Enterprise: Seven Business Innovators and the Empires They Built*. New York: Collins, 2003 (paperback reprint).

Trump, Donald, and Tony Schwartz. *Trump: The Art of the Deal*. New York: Random House, 1987.

Vise, David A., and Mark Malseed. *The Google Story*. New York: Delacorte, 2005.

Wallace, James, and Jim Erickson. *Hard Drive: Bill Gates and the Making of the Microsoft Empire*. New York: Collins, 1993 (paperback reprint).

Welch, Jack, with John A. Byrne. *Jack, Straight from the Gut*. New York: Warner, 2001.

Welch, Jack, and Suzy Welch. *Winning*. New York: Collins., 2005.

Young, Jeffrey S., and William L Simon. *iCon Steve Jobs: The Greatest Second Act in the History of Business*. Hoboken, NJ: Wiley, 2005.

Yunus, Muhammad. *Banker to the Poor: Micro-Lending and the Battle Against World Poverty*. New York: PublicAffairs, 2003 (paperback reprint).

Zook, Chris, with James Allen. *Profit from the Core: Growth Strategy in an Era of Turbulence*. Boston: Harvard Business School Press, 2001.

Websites and Other Resources

These web sites offer a great deal of data and information about the factors that influence business culture Some of these resources are subscription-based services; check with your library to see if they offer access to these services at no charge.

www.businessculture.com

This website offers information on a variety of topics, including business customs, etiquette, and cultural "norms" that shape work life across borders.

http://knowledge.wharton.upenn.edu

The Wharton School (the business school of the University of Pennsylvania) shares its intellectual capital through this website, the school's online business journal. Knowledge@Wharton offers free access to information including analysis of current business trends, interviews with industry leaders and Wharton faculty, and articles based on recent business research.

www.hoovers.com

Research companies and industries; research corporate executives and decision makers.

www.standardandpoors.com

Provider of independent credit ratings, indices, risk evaluation, investment research, data, and valuations.

www.moodys.com

Investing and finance data; economic analysis.

www.bloomberg.com

Breaking financial, business and economic news worldwide.

http://forrester.com/mag/

A magazine published by Forrester Research, Inc., headquartered in Cambridge, Massachusetts.

www.nyse.com

Official site of the New York Stock Exchange.

www.cnnmoney.com

Internet home of *Fortune, Money, Business 2.0,* and *Fortune Small Business,* including the Fortune 500.

www.ssireview.org

The Stanford Social Innovation Review is a publication of the Center for Social Innovation at the Stanford Graduate School of Business.

http://www.shrm.org/
Society for Human Resource Management 1800 Duke Street, Alexandria, Virginia 22314.

www.marketingpower.com/
American Marketing Association—a professional association for marketers.

www.amanet.org/
American Management Association—a professional development association for managers, providing training and networking opportunities.

www.wageproject.org
The WAGE Project, Inc is a 501(c)3 charitable, tax-deductible organization established to end discrimination against women in the American workplace. The website includes resources for information, support and advocacy.

www.aarp.org
A resource for policy, advocacy, information, support and connections pertaining to persons over fifty.

www.valuenewsnetwork.com
"Exploring Tomorrow's Markets, Enterprise, & Investments" is the tagline at this interactive website, which offers resources and information for businesses, government, organizations and individuals on creating value and on the forces and influences shaping value creating in today's environment.

www.wsj.com
Website of the *Wall Street Journal.*

www.nytimes.com
Website of *The New York Times.*

www.forbes.com
Website of *Forbes Magazine.*

www.fastcompany.com
Website of *Fast Company Magazine.*

www.dol.com
Website of the U.S. Department of Labor.

www.sba.gov
Website of the United States Small Business Administration.

www.amanet.org
Website of the American Management Association.

www.marketingpower.org
Website of the American Marketing Association.

www.shrm.org
Website of the Society for Human Resource Management.

www.nawbo.org
    Website of the National Association of Women Business Owners (NAWBO).

www.nwbc.gov
    Website of the National Women's Business Council.

www.marshall.usc.edu
    Accesses the website for the Center for Effective Organizations (resources include seminars, research, working papers, conferences, books and videos).

www.leadertoleader.org
    Website of the Leader to Leader Institute, originally established as the Peter F. Drucker Foundation for Nonprofit Management.

www.inc.com
    This website is a resource for entrepreneurs; also the website of *Inc.* magazine.

Index

Boldface page numbers indicate main entry

ABOUT THE EDITOR

REGINA FAZIO MARUCA is a freelance business writer and editor, specializing in marketing, branding, leadership, and organizational culture. Also a Principal at the Center for Executive Development, she has served as a Senior Editor at the *Harvard Business Review*, reporter and editor at *Boston Business Journal*, and Associate Managing Editor at *New England Business Magazine*, and has conducted interviews with high-profile business leaders for *Fast Company*. Since 2000 she has provided editorial, writing, and research services for authors at such organizations as Harvard Business School, Accenture, the Committee of 200, and Boston University. She is coauthor, with Robert M. Galford, of *Your Leadership Legacy* and editor of *What Managers Say, What Employees Hear* (Praeger, 2006).